Laugh With Me / Cry With Me

Laugh With Me / Cry With Me

Inspiration, Pathos, and Humor from

Ivan Fitzwater

Illustrations by Paul Hudgins

THE
WATERCRESS
PRESS

San Antonio, Texas
1990

First Edition

A Watercress Press book
Published by Evett & Associates, San Antonio, Texas
for
Management Development Institute, Inc.

Library of Congress Catalog Card No. 89-52014

ISBN 0-934955-15-8

Cover design by Paul Hudgins
Printed and bound in the United States of America

To Cecil and Jenny Mae,
Emerson and Martha,
for their constant encouragement
and to Elaine

Contents

Laugh With Me / Cry With Me

STORIES

It's All Right to Cry

I was nine years old and my best friend had just died. His name was Joe and I had gotten him as a puppy. He had disappeared before when a female sent out the siren call of passion, but he had always come back—often in tatters and extremely tired—but he had always returned. This time, though, one day became two, then three. My mother shook her head as if to prepare me for the worst.

We were just a collection of houses along the little country road, not a town or a community with a name. We all knew each other well, too, so the neighbors knew Joe was missing.

Buster Beal found him, but by the time Buster came to tell us, he had two older boys with him. Mom and I were home alone, so we got the news together.

"I'm not sure it's him, he's tore up so bad," Buster said to my mother. "Them dogs done killed some hound and it sure looks like Joe."

I resented the term hound. "He's part cocker," I protested under my breath, but there was no time to deal with their ignorance now. I wanted to go see right away but without seeming anxious in front of the older boys.

"You want to go see if it's Joe?" Buster asked.

"Yeah," I said, trying to sound tough. "Let's go."

My mother wanted me to wait for Dad to come home from

work, but I couldn't wait. I had to know. Besides, waiting would look sissy.

The path through the woods behind our house was familiar. I had shot many an outlaw there. It was also the shortcut to Patrick's Store. Buster and the others went ahead of me a few paces and instead of bullying me as they often did, they were unusually kind and sort of quiet. They had dogs, too, and although Joe was mine, he shared his love with everybody. He played with all of us at the school bus stop in the morning and met us again each evening. Buster and the others loved him, too, of course, but, like me, they couldn't admit it.

The path was worn smooth where it curved around a huge, dead chestnut tree. The air was damp and heavy, making the red clay slippery beneath my bare feet. Suddenly the air was filled with a terrible odor of decaying flesh that seemed to sear my nostrils.

Buster pointed to a spot a few feet off the path and in a low voice said, "Over here."

My heart suddenly clogged my throat, and I fought back tears with every ounce of courage a nine-year-old can muster. It was Joe—his eyes frozen open, blood caked in his thick hair. Flies swarmed as we moved closer.

"That's old Joe, ain't it?" somebody asked. I couldn't answer; I couldn't speak. I wanted to scream, to cry, to run, but men don't do those things. Men are tough. I moved closer. It took all the strength I had, but I knew I must do it. I had to prove to the older boys that I was tough, that I didn't care.

I reached forward with my foot and, as casually as I could, I rolled Joe over. A knot of greasy maggots bubbled like a boiling pot as they were exposed to light and the nauseous stench was overpowering. I turned and started back on the path toward home as if what I had just seen meant nothing to me.

Emerging from the woods, I noticed through blurry eyes that my mother was sitting in a chair under the tree by the smokehouse. Snapping a mess of beans on her lap, she looked up just long enough to get the answer to her unspoken question.

I nodded my head and walked quickly behind the henhouse and out of sight.

I was still sitting there when I heard my father's car pull into the driveway. I couldn't hear what he and Momma were saying, but I knew. In a few minutes, Dad walked up with a shovel in his hand.

"Better show me where he is, Son," he said quietly, his eyes searching mine. I nodded and walked ahead, back along the path into the woods.

My father was a tall man and very strong—he had to be to endure what he had during those awful days of the Depression. In spite of working seven-day weeks, he had lost his farm and had to start over as a carpenter at age 55. With his own hands, he had built the house where we now lived, much of it by lantern light after working all day for someone else. I had never felt afraid when I was with him, but now I did. Suppose I cried when I saw Joe again. What would my father think of me?

I stopped by the path and pointed. Dad walked over, paused a moment, then started to scrape a clearing in the leaves with the shovel. The clay was soft, and soon the hole was big enough for a small dog.

Lifting Joe gently into the grave, he started to push the dirt in with his hands. I felt compelled to move closer I needed to take one last look at the friend who had been my constant companion for most of my life. I wanted to say something, if only "Goodbye," but I knew if I tried to speak I wouldn't be able to hold back the tears.

Suddenly, my father stopped pushing at the dirt. Still kneeling, he leaned back on his heels and took a big red handkerchief out of his pocket and blew his nose. As he looked up at me, I could see tears flowing down his cheeks. My father was crying! I fell to my knees and let my own pent-up emotions pour out. I bawled until my eyes were sore and puffy. We shared the big, red handkerchief, my father and I. Then we walked home in silence.

I cried some more that night, and off and on for several days. But in my grief, my weeping was the therapy that started the healing process which eventually restored me.

Never will I forget Joe, nor any of the other dogs I have shared life with since. But I have been better able to deal with loss since I learned that important lesson beside the path that led to Patrick's Store. I learned that day from a real man:

It's all right to cry.

Miss Nettie Preen
of the Snyder School

A move was on in the late 1930's to close the remaining one-room schools in Montgomery County, Maryland. The one which served the twenty or so farm families in our community was named Snyder School after the creek nearby. There had been excitement there before as the obstreperous students pursued their major goal of running off the teacher, but this year of 1938 would outdo all the rest. It would go down in history not only as the final term for the little school, but also as the year Miss Nettie Preen came to teach and accomplish feats which became legendary.

For most students the Snyder School was all the education they would ever get. After attending grades one through six there, students had the option of riding the school bus to the high school in Gaithersburg or dropping out. Most chose the latter. The building itself was a very simple structure, constructed of wood and painted fire-engine red. The interior was literally a single room with wooden desks bolted to the floor in rows. There was an entry door at the front, and coat hangers along the back divided by a door which led to the two outhouses, one for boys and one for girls. A potbellied wood stove was located in the middle of the room to afford heat in very uneven quantities toward the walls.

The Snyder student body was diverse yet homogeneous. It was diverse in that students from ages five through twenty-one studied in a single room; it was homogeneous in that all the people who attended the school came from a very small geographical area. The strapping farm boys looked upon school as an interlude between strenuous farm chores and a chance to act out their aggression which they could not do at home under the watchful eyes of demanding fathers. To the girls it was a place to gather socially and to gossip and talk about the boys. For both boys and girls it was a place to get together to socialize and overcome the isolation that goes along with farm life.

For teachers it was the Devil's Island of education, a place where you worked temporarily until you earned your way to the big schools in the towns. Teachers who came there were either on their way up or on their way out. To the County School Board it was a test of competency. If you could make it in the one-room school you were worthy of appointment or reinstatement to the big schools in town. It was common to have several teachers in a single year with weeks of vacation in between while the school board selected some unsuspecting soul as a replacement.

Leonard Farnsworth, III, was the teacher chosen to open school in September of 1938. He lasted less than a week. The boys and girls were standing around the school yard when Leonard got off the bus which brought him to Snyder's Creek and picked up the older students who were going to school in town. He was barely nineteen years of age, and when he began the day by addressing the students as "ladies and gentlemen," the big boys in class looked at each other and smiled because they knew he was going to be an easy victory.

The second recess that day, when he went into the boys' out-house, the students wedged a two-by-four into the ground and under the handle of the outhouse door, effectively trapping the teacher in odoriferous confinement. The students probably planned to let him out later, but they became so engrossed in play that when the school bus came by, signaling the end of the day, they went home and left the poor teacher trapped. When a passing farmer heard him screaming that night and freed him at about nine o'clock, Teacher Farnsworth took himself and his career and headed up the road, never to be heard of again.

The second week of school brought a new teacher and a new challenge for the students. This man had obviously been briefed on what had happened to his predecessor. It is still a mystery how he did it, but for three days of his tenure he never went to the outhouse once. Most of the day he spent with his back solidly to the wall and he interfered as little as possible with the students, who proceeded to entertain themselves in various ways. It was Thursday before he had confidence enough to sit down, but that was a mistake because the twenty-six thumbtacks in his seat brought him quickly to his feet and set off a string of oaths that forever compromised his effectiveness as a teacher. His resignation at the end of that week was an act of conscience because of his unseemly language, but to the students it was a disappointment because they felt they hadn't really earned his exodus.

You might think that the parents were disturbed at such a halting start to the school year, but they weren't because this was pretty much what they had expected. Most of them had attended the Snyder School, too, so they were familiar with the selection process which was used to cull the cast-offs that were sent them by the Board of Education. It was a necessary process that had to be pursued until a strong teacher was found who could finish out the year. The parents didn't openly approve of the students' misbehavior and certainly tolerated nothing of the kind at home, but their understanding of the realities, and the code of silence embraced by the students—even the goody-goody ones — combined to support the concept of teacher selection at Snyder School.

On Monday, the third week of school, in this memorable year of 1938, the nineteen students who made up the student body were all present bright and early to meet the new teacher and to assess the new challenge. Most of the girls wore home-made dresses made from colorful muslin feedsacks; the boys wore overalls and workshirts. Virtually every student was barefoot. If such a motley-looking crew were to be seen today, it would be ludicrous. Then it was just the way things were—a normal student body for a one-room country school.

It was a bright, blue September morning as the students awaited the arrival of teacher number three. The seesaws and other playground equipment were idle, as were the hopscotch squares and marble rings. Russell Dowd, a thirteen-year-old, and the three twelve-year-olds who made up his gang leaned against the rail fence that ran along the creek. These were the leaders who decided what mischief should be done, and they stationed themselves near the short driveway to get the first glimpse of the new challenger. They watched the school bus stop by the row of mailboxes that lined the intersection of the roads on the other side of the creek. The bus picked up several high school students who were going to school in town, but no teacher got off. The students were puzzled by this situation and were discussing it as the school bus kicked up a cloud of dust which slowly dissipated as the bus moved farther out of sight.

The boys started to congratulate themselves on the possibility that there would be no teacher, that the word had gotten out that this was a school where nobody could survive. Just as they were about to announce their conclusion to the rest of the students and signal the beginning of play, they noticed another cloud of dust, which heralded an approaching car. As it came into view, they saw a 1932 Model A Ford that appeared to be running without a driver. As it started up the short lane into the school, they could see that there was indeed a driver—a frail-looking little woman who had to tilt her chin upward to see out through the windshield. As Nettie Preen got out of her car, the boys looked at each other and snickered. This was going to be too easy. Russell Dowd put up one finger, predicting the number of days tenure that he foresaw for the new teacher.

To say that Nettie Preen did not look like your ordinary school teacher would be an understatement. She was a short, slender woman, no more than five feet two inches tall and weighing not an ounce over ninety pounds. Her jet black hair was rolled up in a bun on the back of her head. She had rimless glasses perched on a very long nose and a pale complexion that looked almost as white as the gloves she wore. You would think a woman so tiny would attempt to elevate her stature by wearing high-heeled shoes, but Nettie didn't. She wore flat, black shoes with laces that tied and dark hose that extended up her slim legs and rolled up just under the knees. The stern, unsmiling look on her face seemed most compatible with the sharp facial features and her jet black dress. As someone observed later, if you handed her a broom and a tall black hat she'd have looked just like a diminutive witch.

Miss Preen didn't acknowledge any of the students in the school yard. Instead, she took a small briefcase off the seat of her car and marched directly over to the bell that rested on top of a tall pole just in front of the schoolhouse door. She gave a couple of yanks on the rope to signal the beginning of school. Then, without looking to right or left, she marched straight in the front door, out of sight.

The students looked at each other and then to their leader, Russell Dowd. Puzzled and curious, the only thing he could think of doing was to follow the teacher into the building. Of course, all of the other students followed, too.

Immediately, they took their places in the rows of seats and studied this new teacher who seemed completely oblivious to their presence. Miss Preen opened her briefcase, took out her books and a small glass ball filled with clear liquid. In the middle of the glass ball was a statue of George Washington. When the ball was shaken, white flakes circulated through the liquid, making it look like it was snowing on his statue. She shook the ball, stirring up the snow, and put it on the corner of her desk. The students at Snyder School had never seen anything like that before. So rapt was their attention to this strange object, they hardly noticed that Miss Preen immediately started a spelling lesson and everyone in class, including Russell Dowd, was soon writing on a slate.

Before the students knew it, it was recess and they hadn't tried even one prank. Outside, Russell Dowd shrugged it off when he was questioned by saying that, since she was such a small woman, he wanted to make sure that they were no more cruel than needed. After recess, and again after lunch, Miss Preen put them to work so fast they hardly touched the seat of their britches to the desk before they became involved. The afternoon went by fast, with the little teacher pouring on the work and the bewildered students too confused to organize any resistance.

Walking home that afternoon, Russell Dowd and his gang realized that they'd have to get busy if they were going to avoid this kind of hard work. So under Russell's leadership, they decided to get it over with quickly, rather than having a prolonged series of actions to dislodge Nettie Preen. That night the boys each told their parents they were going gigging for fish, but instead, they took hammers and some other tools and met back at the schoolhouse. Then with a bit of ingenious engineering, they proceeded to remove the nails which held the girls' outhouse walls together.

The result of their work that night was a devilish trap for Miss Preen. The roof of the outhouse now was the only thing holding up the walls. They had attached a rope to the top of the roof and put it across a crook in a tree just above the little building so that one pull on the rope would lift the roof, the four sides would fall away and leave nothing but the toilet itself, occupied, for all the world to see.

The word was passed around the playground the next morning, so everybody waited with great anticipation. Miss Preen arrived and, followed by her students, went directly into the schoolhouse. Without a smile she promptly put them to work. They could hardly concentrate, and they would sneak looks at one another as if to ask, "When in the world would Miss Preen have to use the toilet?"

Just before morning recess the great moment arrived. Miss Preen started out to the outhouse while the students were reading their geography lesson. Just as she closed the back door,

Russell Dowd dashed out the front to the tree where the rope was dangling. Giving the other students time to get out so that they could see the spectacle, he tugged at the rope. The rope lifted, the walls fell, and there, in all her glory, was Miss Preen perched on the toilet. A look of shock came across her face, but only for a second. Glancing briefly at the students laughing at her expense, she arose, adjusted her clothing, and walked straight back into the schoolhouse without a word.

No outburst, no screaming, no crying, no threats. The students were confused. Curiosity alone was enough to get them back into their seats and Miss Preen put them right back to work. But, when the usual time for recess came, the teacher called no break. In fact, she worked them right through lunch. It wasn't until about 1:30 in the afternoon that she finally gave in and let them go one by one, boys and girls alike, to the boys' outhouse. That brief period of laughter they had had at the teacher's expense was balanced off by a longer-than-usual day of very hard schoolwork. Later, as the boys walked home from school, they noticed that Miss Preen headed her car in the direction of the Dowd farm.

By the time Russell got home, his father was waiting with a razor strop, a tool box, and some nails. After the strop got its exercise, Russell and his dad went around to the other farms, picked up the boys, and they all spent the evening rebuilding the girls' outhouse. By the next morning when the students arrived, it was as good as new, a monument to Russell Dowd's failure.

There is no question that Russell and his friends had received a severe setback, but they were far from finished. It took several days for them to get up enough courage to try another prank. Just about the time the pain of the razor strop had fully healed, their creativity was again aroused, but, in the interim, they spent more than a week of hard work on their lessons.

Their second try to dislodge Miss Preen was rather mild compared to the first. The boys' scheme involved removing the pins from the hinges on the front door so that when she touched the latch the next morning, the entire door would fall on top of her. Fortunately, when she arrived, Miss Preen realized what was happening in time and stepped aside as the door crashed onto the front porch, narrowly missing six-year-old Joanie May. Waiting only long enough for the dust to settle, Miss Preen lifted her long skirt, stepped up onto the door, and walked right into the school with students following. No mention was made of the door lying on the front porch and the autumn chill that came into the room. No one dared even to open their mouths unless they were spoken to.

That afternoon when Miss Preen seemed to be heading her car in the direction of the Dowd house, the boys raced to flag her down.

"Miss Preen, Miss Preen," they gasped, out of breath. "Please, Miss Preen, we'll fix the door! Please come back, Miss Preen. Don't worry; we'll fix the door right this minute. OK?"

Another time, when they put the gunnysack over the top of the chimney and smoke poured out of the stove and into the classroom, Miss Preen simply reached into her desk drawer and pulled out the white gloves she always wore for driving. Holding them across her nose provided an effective filtration mask, and she paid no heed to the smoke that was filling the room, causing the children to cough and their eyes to burn.

Finally, when they could stand it no longer, the students bolted from the room into the clean air outside. Russell, remembering the razor strop, scampered up onto the roof, unplugged the chimney, and the smoke quickly ascended from the classroom. Nettie Preen kept an exact accounting of the time spent in this vicarious activity and kept her students that much longer at the end of the day. When anxious parents began to arrive to see what was keeping their children from getting home on time, Miss Preen explained that she had not been able to teach for an hour or so because Russell and the others had plugged up the chimney, but she encouraged the parents to talk with Mr. Dowd if they had any complaints about the length of the school day. Alas, the razor strops were busy again that night!

Russell Dowd and the other boys were just about ready to give up their attempts to rid the school of this teacher. All they had gotten so far for their efforts to drive her off was total defeat and humiliation from the other students, not to mention several of the most effective whippings they had ever had. Maybe it was time to take another approach. Perhaps confrontation was not the answer. By golly, whenever the teacher starts getting the upper hand, the obvious response is truancy, they decided.

It was at this point that this writer got a chance to be an observer at one of the most celebrated events that ever happened in that small community. Russell Dowd and the other boys had decided to skip school the next day and although at five I was not old enough to go to first grade, I was invited to go fishing with them, even swimming if the weather got hot enough.

The next day was one of the warmest I can remember for the end of October in Maryland. I went along with the boys to school but, stopping short of the schoolhouse, we went straight for the swimming hole. Pausing by the bridge, we took out our hickory stick fishing poles from the place where we kept them hidden so we would not have to carry them back and forth. Around the poles we had wrapped some white string and a cork which floated on top of the water and bobbled whenever we got a bite. As we walked, we located several cow pies, turned them over to capture some nice big earthworms, then baited our hooks and waited in the warm sunlight.

Although we were only a short distance from school, the bushes which grew along the bank of the stream concealed our position, so we knew we were safe. The morning stretched on—the fish were not biting—so we ate our lunch early and looked around for something else to occupy our time.

Then Joe Foray suggested that we go swimming, but the rest of us wondered whether the water was too cold on this late autumn day. What ensued was a match to see if anyone would have the courage to go into the chilly water. So it was decided that I would be the guinea pig and, urged—no, vigorously pressed—by the older boys, I stripped naked, and trembling at every step, I tiptoed into the stream. Not to be outdone by the youngest of the group, the others soon followed and it wasn't long before we had adjusted to the temperature of the water and were laughing and frolicking with joyous abandon.

Suddenly there was a deathly silence. I turned around and there, standing on the bank at the edge of the stream, was Miss Nettie Preen! Five naked, scared boys lowered their eyes from her piercing stare and ducked down into the water up to their chins.

"Russell Dowd," she scolded in her high voice, "you come out of that water right now. I'm taking you back to school. Do you hear me? I said, 'Right now!'"

"But, Miss Preen, you gotta let me get my clothes on," Russell responded. "I ain't wearing no swimming suit."

"You should have thought of that before you got in there. You come right now or I'm coming in there to get you."

We were all shivering now, but it wasn't from the cold water. Russell was going to defy Miss Preen. We had seen before what her wrath could do.

Miss Preen stared and Russell stood motionless. Then she did something which shocked and amazed us all. She kicked off her shoes, and started into the water, lifting her dress gradually to keep it just above the water level. If the stream had been much deeper I think she would have drowned, as short as she was. But she was able to reach Russell while her nose and mouth were still above the water level. Russell Dowd was too panicked to move. When she got within reach, she took a good grip on his right ear, turned slowly, and started back toward the bank with Russell in tow. By the time Miss Preen had slipped back into her shoes, she was dragging along a boy bigger then she was, who was naked as a jaybird and crying.

She tugged him along in the direction of the school, completely oblivious to his pleadings that he be allowed to get his clothes. Russell could see the line of students along the fence by the schoolhouse. He knew that in just a minute or two he was going to be facing them, wearing exactly what he did when he came into this world. I'm sure he could have stopped her if he had tried because he was bigger than she was, but I guess he realized if he tried to fight back he would first have to remove his hands from where he was using them to protect his modesty, and he probably would have also lost an ear. His pleadings grew more intense.

They were now about a hundred yards from the school. Miss Preen stopped and looked straight into the eyes of Russell Dowd. He stopped his crying and studied her to see what her next act might be.

"Russell, get down on your knees."

He instantly obeyed.

"If I let you go back and get your clothes, will you promise that you'll come to school every day and not skip another time for the rest of the year?"

"Yes, ma'm. I surely will. I'll be there every day and I'll even make sure them other boys don't miss."

"Will you ever pull another prank on me, or do anything to disrupt my school?"

"No, ma'm. I never will. I cross my heart and hope to die; I never will."

There was a moment or so of silence as if Miss Preen was deciding whether or not to accede to his pleas. Then suddenly she let him go and started walking toward the schoolhouse. Russell Dowd ran back to the bushes and put on his clothes so fast he almost beat her back into the classroom.

Nettie Preen completed her year of teaching at the Snyder School without any further challenge on the part of anyone. But the Snyder School was closed that year, and the children were transferred to larger schools as part of the consolidation effort to provide more modern education. When she retired after a long and distinguished career as a respected educator, hundreds of Miss Preen's former students came to the retirement party to show their gratitude. The master of ceremonies was a tall, rustic-looking farmer by the name of Russell Dowd. He said many fine things about the guest of honor but there was a tear in his eye when he stated firmly that the greatest desire of his life was that his children could have a teacher like Miss Nettie Preen.

All present nodded in agreement.

Blind Faith

Sadie Welsh stood at graveside in the Methodist cemetery to say goodbye to Samuel, her husband of forty years. He had been her lover, her constant companion, the father of her children, and a man she had never seen. Sadie was blind from birth and so was Samuel.

It was not hard to develop a schedule of visitation because the two old people were so well known and loved by all the church people. I willingly took my place on the schedule, even though I did not look forward to what I assumed would be a rather sad experience.

I stopped my car in front of the Welsh home and spent a moment or two trying to build up my courage for the task at hand. I really had not gotten to know the Welshes very well, only through our Sunday meetings at church. They were always smiling and full of optimism, but that was when they were together.

I pushed the doorbell and waited. Soon I heard the tapping of a cane on the tile of the foyer. A very friendly voice asked, "Who is it?" I gave my name and she opened the door. I told her I had stopped by from the church just to see how she was doing.

"Yes, I know you. You are the very tall man from church."

For a moment I though she could see the quizzical look on my face when I wondered how she knew I was tall. She answered my unasked question by telling me that when you are blind, you are very sensitive to where a voice comes from. In my case, it had always come from above her head.

She led the way to a very bright and cheerful living room and proceeded to chatter about things at the church and some of the things that she had been doing around the house. Her attitude was not at all what I had expected. From what I understood, Samuel's death had so crushed her that she was in a morose state and almost uncommunicative. This wasn't the situation at all. She was upbeat, happy, optimistic and seemed anxious to have someone listen to her.

"You sure I'm not boring you with all of my chatter?"

"Not at all. I'm very interested in what you have been doing and I'm very pleased to see that you are in such fine spirits."

"I was about as low as you could get the first couple of weeks after Samuel's death, but after everybody left, I had a chance to think about what was really happening. I've got it pretty well figured out now. And I am at peace with myself and with the world.

"You know, it's easier for blind people to adjust if sighted people would just go ahead and act normally. When you say it's a beautiful day and talk about the bright sunshine, we know exactly what you mean. We can't see the light, but we can feel the warmth and we sense the pleasant feeling that it gives the people around us. Did you ever stop to realize that the best part of a beautiful day is the sunshine that it brings out of people's hearts?"

I answered that I had never really seen it that way before.

"That's because you've never seen it through the eyes of a blind person. We smell the flowers probably more sensitively than you do, but we see the flowers through the happiness that comes forth as others around us see them. I really don't know what a tree looks like, but it must be something beautiful because people have happiness in their voice when they talk about a tree. You can enjoy the sight of the tree, while I can enjoy the happiness that comes through to me as you look at it."

The afternoon was wearing on into evening now as we continued our conversation. Sadie apologized for keeping me so long, but I explained to her that I was enjoying the visit very much.

"Let me warm up your coffee one more time and then you must get home to your family."

I did not notice that it was getting pretty dark in the room until she went over and turned on the light.

"I bet you wonder how I knew that it was getting dark in the room. Well, you see, when you are blind, you develop a tremendous sense of time.

"They tell me that most couples grow apart as they get on toward middle age and then older. In many of those cases the differences get so great that the two people can't even stand each other any more. It wasn't that way with Samuel and me and maybe it's because of this unique situation of our blindness. We were together every minute of every day and never once did we get bored with each other. We looked forward to every day and we constantly looked for ways to help each other, particularly as we got older and we got a little more feeble. Don't let that smile that he always had on his face fool you. At times he could get a little grouchy, but it was just his way of letting me know that he needed a little more love and reassurance."

I finished my coffee and thanked Sadie for a very pleasant afternoon. She told me how grateful she was for the care of the people from the church and particularly for my taking so long to listen to a talkative old woman.

"Are you sure you're going to be all right here now by yourself? Is there anything else I can get for you?"

"No, I'll be just fine. You go right along and give my love to your fine family. I've got a number of things I've got to do and, you see, there isn't much time."

I had started to open the door, but when she made that statement I paused and turned to her. "Is there some place you have to go? Are you going to need transportation?"

She laughed and said, "No, where I'm going I won't need any transportation."

I swallowed hard as I realized what she meant.

"For the first couple of weeks after Samuel died, I was wallowing in self-pity and I was being unrealistic. I'm as old as he was and my health is failing, too. One of us had to stay behind for a little bit to get some things taken care of. But this separation is only temporary."

I muttered something to the effect that she shouldn't be talking that way but she interrupted my statement.

"You don't understand. I'm speaking happy thoughts. These

few weeks are the longest that we've been apart in over forty years. I miss that man too much, but pretty soon now we'll be back together again. And this time we won't be blind. Oh, it concerns me a little that I might not look just the way he's pictured me, but then he may not turn out to be the handsome man I've always thought he was. I figure after all we've shared together, any little problems in that regard can be overcome. I just can't wait for us to spend eternity together because I sure do miss that man."

I gave her hand a little squeeze and put my arm around her shoulder. I had a lump in my throat so I couldn't speak. I closed the door behind me and walked out toward my car. The light beside her steps switched on so I could see, and as I turned I noticed the light in the living room went out.

I never saw Sadie again because she died before it came my turn to visit again. As I sat at her funeral service, my mind reflected back on our conversation of that afternoon. I wondered to myself if she got all the things done that she wanted to do before she had to go. I suspect she may have even left a few of them undone, because she was so anxious to be reunited with Samuel. She left behind with me, and with others who knew her during those latter days, a totally new meaning of the phrase "blind faith."

The Cornfield Experience

Gravel pelted the fenders of our 1938 Plymouth as my father and I hurried along the dirt road to Bailey's farm. Daylight was just breaking on a very humid, August, dog-day in Maryland. As any thirteen-year-old, I yearned for sleep and tried to doze as we rattled along. It seemed like just another day of work to be endured. Instead, it was to be the beginning of an experience which would teach me much about myself and the world in 1944.

My father was a carpenter and painter and I worked as his helper during school vacations. But today we were going to help harvest corn for the silos on Bailey's dairy farm. We had just finished painting the interior of the dairy barns and Mr. Bailey was short of help in that war year. He asked if we might help with the harvest and he would pay painter wages, which was a concession of major proportion. It sounded like fun to me—a change of pace from the hard life of an apprentice painter. How little I knew and how much I had to learn!

My father was assigned to the relatively high prestige job of a stacker on one of the wagons which hauled the stalks of corn from the field to the storage silos. Corn from the wagons was then fed into a chopping machine which pulverized the heavy stalks and literally blew them up a chute where the silage fell into the fifty-feet tall silos. This high protein food was the diet staple for a large herd of dairy cows.

My job assignment was not as prestigious. I was part of a team of four choppers who cut the corn by hand and put it in piles to be picked up by the teams of haulers. The tall stalks, some seven feet high, were cumbersome and heavy. They had to be cut and cradled in the arm until enough were collected for a sizeable pile. The aim was to have large bundles and few piles, so the wagons could make as few stops as possible. When I had chopped enough stalks and was nearing the point of dumping my bundle, it felt as if I were hugging a tree.

The other three members of my team were tall, black men who were regular farm laborers. I guessed they were in their late forties or early fifties, too old for service in World War II. Years of rugged farm work had given them rippling muscles and what seemed to me unbelievable strength.

Their disdain for me was immediate and very obvious; they talked among themselves but never to me. They were stronger and faster workers and I struggled to keep up. They would sit down and rest, and just as I would catch up, they would start again, so I would get no rest. They had water, which I had not anticipated the need for, but offered me none. They laughed at my stumbling along with the heavy bundles which they hefted easily.

At noon they went off to lunch without saying a word. I sat under a tree, ate my bag of lunch, and pondered my situation. The sunburn on my nose and forehead began to sting. I thought to myself, "Even the sun in unfair; it burns me but not them. Why won't they give me a chance? I'm doing my best. Just because I can't keep up is no excuse for their cruelty."

When dusk and quitting time finally arrived I was exhausted. My neck was bleeding from the cuts of the sharp blades of corn. Sweat irritated the cuts which, along with the sunburn, made me miserable. That night I could hardly sleep because of muscle cramps, so I had to sleep curled up in a ball.

Facing the second day was one of the hardest challenges I have ever experienced. I was tempted to tell my father I was sick when he awakened me. Somehow, I got the courage to return to what was sure to be another day of punishment from my team members.

"We don't need to take our lunch today," my father said. "I learned yesterday that they furnish dinner for all harvest hands."

I regretted this because the only moments of reprieve from the men's cruelty the day before had been when they left for an hour while I sat alone in the shade and ate the sandwiches my mother had packed for me.

The morning was just like the day before, but at least I was prepared. I had a handkerchief around my neck to prevent cuts, a straw hat for the sun, and water in a canteen. The men continued to make fun of me constantly and did nothing to acknowledge my attempts to be a hard worker. It was pure luck that I saw the hornets' nest just before I would have hacked it with my corn cutter. They were used to such things and were on the alert, but they didn't expect me to be. They were obviously disappointed that I avoided being stung by the aggressive insects.

At noon the men went off to catch the wagon which took the field hands to dinner. They looked surprised to see me follow them because I had not done so the day before. I lay back on a load of corn stalks and instantly fell asleep as the rumbling wagon took us to the main house for dinner. The clanging dinner bell awakened me and I joined the line of men headed toward the row of wash basins just outside the main house.

Each man washed his hands and face in the basin and then emptied it so the next could refill it from the spigot. A roll of coarse paper served as a universal towel. I waited in line, washed my hands and threw out the water in the basin.

Dinner for harvest hands is a monstrous meal. Stacks of fried chicken, mounds of beans, and heaps of yeast rolls made up the feast. I filled my plate and followed the men to tables under a grove of maple trees. I did not notice that all of the white workers took their food to a screened porch on the back of the main house. The meal was a strictly segregated event, breached only by my inadvertent action. The stares of disbelief by the black workers finally garnered my attention. I felt out

of place, but it was too late now. I had eaten most of my dinner, so I remained with the group.

That afternoon the most amazing change occurred in the
behavior of the four. Their actions turned from disdain of me
to friendliness and they welcomed me into their clique. We
actually performed as a team, sharing laughter, sweat, and
fatigue. When I got behind, they came over and cut stalks for
me until I caught up. We rested together and shared water from
a dipper made out of a gourd. I was dumbfounded, but glori-
ously happy at the change.

We took a week and a half to complete the harvest of the
silage corn. I was sorry when the harvest was over and I believe
my teammates were, too. But it took the passing of years to
give me the wisdom to understand what had happened in that
cornfield. Those men were angry and they rejected me, not
because of my halting performance, but because I was white.
Being young made me vulnerable, a safe target for their pent-
up feelings.

I would love to be able to say that my action that day in bridging a racial barrier was a conscious protest. It was not; it was an accident. I would love to be able to say that the next day many whites joined us under the maple trees. They did not, not one. What did happen was in myself and the other three on the corn chopper team. For a brief moment, we shared an oasis of brotherhood and I saw a glimpse of a world that was destined to come about in my lifetime.

The Miracle Cure

"Oh da ladi hee, oh da ladi hee." Adolphus Garner leaned back against the walnut tree and sang to himself. His horse, tied to the medicine wagon, dozed inattentively as "Doctor" Adolphus sang a nonsensical potpourri of bits and pieces of songs from a limited repertoire, energized by his drunken condition.

"It was sure a damn good day back there in Rockville. Those suckers bought a hundred bottles of my tonic."

He interrupted his singing and mumbling with outbursts of laughter which echoed back from the surrounding hills. As he laughed he threw back his head revealing stained yellow teeth, except for the one missing in front. Tobacco juice collected on his chin and ran in eddies down his neck. Adolphus was pleased with himself. Now it was time to relax and enjoy his success by singing and laughing before fatigue caused him to stretch out on a blanket under the stars until morning, when the challenge of another town would lie ahead.

Business was likely to remain good because his product filled a need. The poor and God-fearing farm people had to work hard in 1915, just to make a living. Other than church on Sunday, there was little but work. Dr. Adolphus sold them a tonic for their health, but to these teetotaling people it was their cocktail hour. The ounce of tonic adults took each evening was 160 proof alcohol with a little sugar and food dye. It stimulated the appetite, encouraged restful sleep, and warded off a variety of unnamed diseases.

The beauty of it for Dr. Adolphus was that people started taking the tonic and found it very hard to stop. Some needed boosters at noon and in the morning to prevent impending ill health. Even the preacher's wife found it necessary to increase the dosage as frailness came upon her at middle age.

Adolphus was about to give in to sleep when he was suddenly confronted by Amos Harns.

"Doc, you gotta help me! Everybody swears by your medicine. I've got a problem that's scaring me senseless."

Adolphus sat up and squinted at the lantern being held close to his face. He pushed it away with his hand and said, "What's ailing you, boy? Can't you see I'm fixin' to sleep?"

"I'm sorry, Dr. Adolphus, but this can't wait. My strength is gone out of my body. Only you can help me."

Amos did not have great intellect, but he had a body that resembled a Greek god. Tall and muscular, he had not an ounce of fat on his body. Amos could chop wood all day and dance to fiddle music all evening and never tire.

The highlight of his year was when the carnival came to town. There was a test of strength, a carnival attraction at which Amos excelled in an incomparable way. A sledge hammer was handed to any man who paid ten cents. If he could slam the hammer down on a treadle hard enough to propel a metal cylinder up a track and ring a bell, the man won two cigars. Amos never failed. He gathered quite a crowd every year, saved his money, rang the bell on every try, and relished the attention this gave him.

"Doc, something's took away my strength, I tell you. Last night I couldn't ring the bell. Everybody walked away and some of them was laughing. I need some of your medicine to get back my strength."

Adolphus knew his medicine would do no good, but he also did not want to be exposed as a fraud. He hit upon a plan which might at least buy him some time. "Son, I can see you are in a bad situation. I can see you need my help, but you got to promise me you won't abuse what I'm going to show you."

Adolphus knew what the carnival man had done. A screw on the lever which propelled the metal cylinder up the track was adjustable. If some strong man started winning a lot of cigars, a few turns on the adjustment made it impossible to ring the bell.

"I'm going to give you a bottle of medicine. It has powers that even I hate to think about. Take a teaspoonful—no more— any time you need super strength. But before you use the power it gives, stop and pray to the Lord that you will succeed. If the Lord don't agree, nothing works, not even this powerful medicine."

Adolphus climbed up into his wagon, poured a bottle full of the white lightning, and added a food dye which turned the liquid bright green. Then he brought the bottle back to Amos.

"Remember, boy, use it only in emergency situations and always ask the Lord to bless your intentions."

The next day Adolphus went back to Rockville early and stopped by the carnival tents just outside of town. None of the carnival people were awake at the early hour of Adolphus' visit. His mission was quickly accomplished. Adolphus knew that Amos would be waiting for the carnival to open that evening so he went to adjust the bell-ringer attachment to make his medicine work and prevent future charges of fraud. A few turns of the adjusting lever assured that anyone could ring the bell. His work done, Adolphus quickly left town.

It was nearly a year before Dr. Adolphus Garner returned to Rockville. Some of his ardent customers had to turn to other salesmen for tonic, rather than chance exposure. Adolphus had avoided his regular circuit because he wasn't sure that his plan for Amos had worked and he feared the wrath that disappointment might have caused. He was much relieved to learn that Amos was indeed at the carnival early that night and that his first blow caused the metal object to decapitate the amusement device. The bell was blown from the top of the track by one strike from Amos' hammer, much to the delight of the spectators.

Amos heard the news of Adolphus' return and was smiling broadly as he rushed up to his wagon, grabbed his hand, and said, "Am I glad to see you! I need some more of that medicine before you leave town. It's a miracle, for sure, the good that can be done with that powerful medicine."

Adolphus eyed Amos cautiously to be sure he was serious, though it was unlikely with Amos' intelligence that he would be anything but simple and honest. "He still ain't discovered the truth," Adolphus muttered to himself.

Adolphus hung a "Gone to Lunch" sign on his wagon and gestured with his head for Amos to follow him to the outhouse behind the saloon. They sat down on a two-seater so they could talk without arousing the attention of townspeople who were attracted by the Doc's wagon.

"Tell me, boy. How did you use that medicine? Did you do like I said?" asked Adolphus.

"Yes, sir, I sure enough did. I took one teaspoon of that stuff and my strength came right back. I hit that bell so hard it knocked the top off and they had to close up the darn thing for the rest of the carnival."

"That's fine, boy. Now what did you do with the rest of it? Why do you need more?"

"I only used it for good things and emergencies. And it worked every time."

"What do you mean, boy?"

"Well, I hid that bottle real good after I learned of its great power. I didn't plan to use it again. But then in June I heard about Mrs. Trainer about to die of cancer before she got to see her daughter graduate from high school. That seemed a shame, hard as she worked to raise that kid by herself. I took the bottle over and told her about its power. We prayed, then she took a teaspoonful and got up off her deathbed and even went to graduation when she hadn't even walked for two months. She died the next day peaceful as could be.

"Then there was Josh Wilson who had to take a test for law school that same month. He's a hard worker but our school cain't keep up with them big city schools. Josh was scared 'til I prayed with him and gave him a spoon of that medicine. Heck, he got one of the highest scores.

"Then the high school basketball team was getting whupped by a team of bigger boys until I got to the coach at halftime. We put a little in the water bucket and got the whole team to pray and then take a drink. They come back in the second half and won by ten points.

"But I mighta done wrong on one, Doc."

"What do you mean, boy?" Adolphus looked at Amos suspiciously.

"Sam Olson said his bull wasn't doing, well, you know, Doc. He wasn't doin' what he was supposed to. I probably shouldn't of, but I told Sam about the medicine and gave him a spoonful for his bull. I guess it didn't work because there don't seem to be any more calves over at his place. I did hear that Mrs. Olson is expecting though, and this surprised me 'cause I thought both of them was beyond child-bearin' age."

"Did you do anything else with it, boy?"

Adolphus opened the outhouse door and started back toward the wagon as if he expected little to remain of Amos's story.

"I did use it a couple of times for myself, Doc. The night that early freeze was a-coming, I had 100 bushels of tomatos in the field which would have all been ruined unless I could pick 'em and git 'em inside. Everybody else was in the same fix, so there was no help. Heck, nobody will believe I did it by myself, but I did. I picked 100 bushels of tomatos in one night and saved my crop.

"Then when the Collins girl went into a coma and the snow was four feet deep in January, she had to be got to a hospital from her place or die. Not even a horse team could go out in that stuff. After I prayed over it, I took a teaspoonful of medicine and carried her ten miles, held her over my head as I tromped in that deep snow.

"And I was tempted to use it a couple of nights last fall, but I didn't. You know how hard the work is during planting season and me all tired in the evening and married less than a year. But I didn't think it right to pray over something like that, so I let it pass."

"Yeah, boy. That wouldn't have been right," Adolphus agreed. "But what you need more for unless you are expecting some emergencies? Is that it, boy?"

"Naw, Doc. That ain't it exactly. You see, the County Judge is running that new thing called a draft board. He says any man without kids got to go over and fight them Germans. Now, Doc, I ain't normally feared of nothing, but I am a little scared of this. It's a long way over there and I ain't rightly sure what a German is. I begin to feel kinda the way I did that night when I lost my strength and couldn't ring that bell.

"I figure a little of that medicine will help me get this war over a lot sooner. I figure once I find where them Germans is, I'll pray a little and take some medicine and then git the job done."

The events of the next two years caused even Adolphus to wonder what he had actually put in that bottle. Amos Harns survived the war and came home one of the most decorated heroes in America.

Montgomery County, Maryland, was fast changing from a collection of little farming communities to suburbs of Washington, D.C. The medicine drummers gave way to modern medicine as the rural people became more enlightened.

Adolphus died from the extended use of his own concoctions. Amos Harns continued to farm but was never again capable of heroic feats. He became less sure of himself and people speculated on why this self-assured hero of a man had become withdrawn. No one ever knew for sure because Amos never revealed his use of the miracle cure.

The Good Church People

Charlie was a gentle, kind man, probably about forty-five years old but no one knew for sure. Nobody knew him very well at all. They thought he worked at some kind of manual labor, but about that they weren't sure either. He wasn't very smart, but he was, as they say, harmless enough.

No one quite remembers when he started attending church—he just seemed to always have been there. Every Sunday he came and sat quietly in the pew and after service left quietly without speaking to anyone. He had a friendly, almost silly smile, but because of his lack of assertiveness he never sought out others nor was he sought out by them. An old brown checkered sport coat, baggy pants, white sox, and brown shoes were his inevitable wardrobe.

If this had been a sophisticated, big city church, Charlie would have stood out even more. But in this tiny church in a small town he was less of an oddity. Most people here were poor but proud to be a member of the flock. Their faith was reinforced by fiery evangelistic sermons delivered by preachers who knew no shades of gray. The paths to heaven and hell were well marked. The everyday activities of life became road signs to be read by the faithful.

Reverend Meems gave his annual Serve Your Church sermon. Never was he more forceful and motivating. Laggards shifted uneasily in their seats until, overcome with guilt, they committed to whatever assignment the Reverend had on the block.

Even passive Charlie was not immune to the persuasive rhetoric. An additional usher was needed to fill out the complement of men who showed worshippers to their seats and took up the morning offering. Charlie surprised everyone, perhaps even himself, when he stood to answer the call of Reverend Meems. Eyebrows were raised particularly by those already on the team of ushers. This job had a measure of prestige and the veterans generally chose replacements when vacancies occurred on rare occasions. But there he stood. How could anyone do less than welcome him to the team?

Charlie did well as a novice usher in spite of the less than enthusiastic feelings of his fellow ushers. His intense effort made up for the hesitating assistance of his colleagues. There were a few minor bumbles and the predictable "I told you so" smiles from the congregation, but nothing sufficient to cause him to lose his position. Some were on the verge of accepting Charlie in spite of his bizarre dress and tentative performance. Then there was that shocking development.

It was probably motivated by jealousy, but Charlie was under intense scrutiny by the other ushers, particularly Samuel Worth. It was Samuel who observed Charlie putting his hand into his pocket just before the collection plates were given to the head usher to be taken to the altar during the Doxology. Could he be stealing from the offering plate? Was that the reason he had brazenly pushed himself on the others?

The word of Charlie's indiscretion spread quickly through the congregation. They shook their heads in disbelief as each told another in strict confidence. Most volunteered that they had suspected Charlie all along, so, heartsick as they were, they were not surprised.

The evidence thus far was circumstantial but in the minds of most it was incontrovertible and quite sufficient. After all, he had put his hand in his pocket while taking up the collection! What possible reason could there be for this except to pilfer money? Still, the action which would have to be taken would require more than circumstantial evidence.

Samuel Worth devised the plan and the others quickly agreed. The money gathered each Sunday was counted in the church office right after the service. Charlie was invited to help count it. All paper money was marked in the upper left-hand corner with a small star, stamped with the rubber stamper used in the Sunday School kindergarten. Two church officials counted the money in advance. Charlie was left alone with the money and then it was recounted by the officials. The recount showed ten dollars missing.

Charlie protested his innocence as best he could with his limited intelligence, but in vain. Only the good hearts of these Christian people kept them from filing criminal charges. Charlie cried when they told him he could no longer usher or even attend this church. He left in shame and disgrace, possibly giving up the only thing in his life which gave it meaning.

No one ever heard of Charlie again. He was the source of gossip for many months but he never violated his banishment. Some said he just left town. Some speculated that he committed suicide but no one knew for sure or ever tried to find out.

The church prospered under Reverend Meems and grew in size. In time, more space was needed which meant an addition of a new sanctuary and a lot of remodeling of the old building. The work didn't take long because everybody united behind the effort.

Samuel Worth and all of the elders were there to hear the report of the architect and contractor. "We are pleased to report that the work is completed according to your instructions. There were no unusual problems and I see no reason why you will not enjoy these new facilities," reported the builder. "By the way, you have ten dollars coming to you as a refund. When we were remodeling the church office we found this ten dollar bill which had fallen down between the baseboard and the wall."

The laugh which the builder expected didn't come as the church leaders stared at a wrinkled ten dollar bill with an odd star in the upper left-hand corner.

Waldo Hostetler's
Prize Pumpkin

Waldo Hostetler was born and raised on the farm that he now owned. When his parents died, he and his wife and family continued a tradition of farming established by his German parents and grandparents. He was totally dedicated to farming and not much interested in what was going on around him in the outside world. The two or so years he had spent in grammar school were not sufficient to pique his interest in local affairs, much less world affairs. Besides, his farm was located in the most rural and isolated area of a sparsely inhabited county, which was Montgomery County, Maryland, in the late 1930's. Waldo was not prepared for the fate that was about to thrust him into the headlines and then send him crashing back to earth.

The small farm where the Hostetlers lived was located adjacent to a gravel county road, leading into the small hamlet of Poolesville. Trips to town were rare so there was minimum contact with the outside world. The traffic on the county road consisted in those days of a school bus and a mailman who delivered everything from baby chicks to that highlight of the year known as the "Sears Roebuck Wish Book."

Waldo was what was called a strapping man—robust, big-boned, and ruddy from hours of work in the out-of-doors. His head looked almost square, like a block of wood sitting on two broad shoulders. His chin was square, too, and jutted out above a very large Adam's apple. It was said that at butchering time he didn't even use a block and tackle to hoist the hogs. He could lift a two-hundred-pound carcass right up on the pole all by himself.

Waldo's farm was barely a hundred acres, small by comparison with most of the others around him. But because of his hard work and his frugal ways, he was able to make a pretty good living. He produced virtually everything that his family needed to eat. His wife made clothes for Waldo, herself, and the children. Nothing went to waste and no expenditures were made unnecessarily. While other farmers were buying fancy new fertilizers, Waldo was careful to keep the manure which was cleaned out of the stables. By stacking it up and letting the chemicals work during the winter, he had his own ready supply of fertilizer by springtime. He then put it in a manure-spreader and applied it to the fields. There was a large vegetable garden, a small orchard, and walnut trees. A small wooded section provided fuel for heat and cooking. It was a compact little operation which required a lot of hard work but rewarded the farmer and his family with independence.

Indulgence in anything for pure pleasure was rare. Sunday was church day, and except for the required chores, the family spent most of the day with the few families who made up the congregation of the fundamentalist Evangelical Church. The younger kids went to school but socializing beyond that was almost entirely with the other farmers who attended the church. Waldo did permit one radio to be in the house, but that was only for family listening, mostly to religious programs, and then only a couple of hours each night. This kept the family from being distracted with too much pleasure, and it also saved the batteries from wearing out so frequently. When the chores were all done the family considered it quite a treat to sit around a coal oil lamp and listen to programs coming from WFMD in Frederick. Then when atmospheric conditions were right, they listened to stations in Washington, D.C. But events were about to occur in the coming autumn of 1938 which would interrupt this tranquil scene and change Waldo Hostetler forever.

In the spring of the year Waldo had applied a heavier than normal amount of his barnyard fertilizer to the cornfield which was located at the front of the farm and just beside the county road. The impact on that year's corn crop was tremendous. The yardstick of "knee high by the Fourth of July" was exceeded by several inches of growth. The other farmers who occasionally passed the field marveled at the tall stalks of corn so early in the summer.

This same rich soil was about to produce another prize crop. To make maximum use of the land it was common practice to plant pumpkins between the rows of corn just after the corn had been thinned and cultivation had removed the weeds. When the corn was cut and put in shocks in autumn, the bright yellow and orange pumpkins were collected and used for a variety of purposes. Mrs. Hostetler would select some of the best ones to make pumpkin pies for the family and for the church covered-dish suppers. The kids used a few to make Halloween jack-o'-lanterns and the others were chopped into parts and thrown into the hog pens to provide a real treat and diet supplement for the swine. This year the fertile soil produced not only a tremendous corn crop, but also some of the largest pumpkins ever seen in the county.

There was one spot in the field that seemed to produce pumpkins even larger than the rest. It was probably the place where Waldo's manure-spreader had slipped a cog in the chain drive because there had obviously been a big application of fertilizer at this one spot. It also happened that this spot was located right beside the county road, so the extra large pumpkins were in full view of all passersby. You couldn't miss them and particularly the one right in the middle, the largest of the lot. Waldo was so fascinated by the size of this huge pumpkin that he decided to let it grow on up until frost, just to see how large it would get. After all the other pumpkins were harvested, the one great pumpkin remained and continued to grow in full view of the county road.

People in town started to talk about Waldo's great pumpkin

and sightseers began to make trips out the county road to see for themselves. A reporter for the Rockville *Gazette* heard about the large pumpkin and came out and took a picture, thus calling attention to it throughout the county. Waldo's farm was becoming a tourist attraction and he didn't know whether to feel pleased or violated.

When the county extension agent came out to see the huge fruit he immediately insisted that Waldo enter the pumpkin in the high school agricultural fair. Waldo was reluctant, but he was also proud, so at the urging of his family and some of the church people, he hauled the pumpkin up to the high school gym for the day-long fair. In truth, he was beginning to enjoy the notoriety and rationalized his feeling of pride on the grounds that the pumpkin was really the Lord's doing. It would not violate his fundamentalist church convictions to be the instrument that helped demonstrate the Creator's power to grow pumpkins.

Waldo's great pumpkin was the showpiece of the agricultural fair. This meant more publicity, more celebrity status for Waldo, and also an invitation to take the great pumpkin to the statewide fair at Timonium, just outside the city of Baltimore. This was a big step for Waldo because he had never done much traveling. The urging of his friends and the obligation which he had incurred as a local winner tipped the scales in favor of making the trip. Soon he was busy doing all the things necessary for a trip of seventy miles. He figured his Model A Ford pickup would make the distance all right, but then he would have to have a place to stay and proper clothes worthy of the owner of a potentially statewide-winning pumpkin.

Waldo and his wife decided that rather than wear homemade clothes, he would instead wear the suit that he had bought at Goodwill to attend his uncle's funeral. The fact that the suit had been bought many years before when he was a bit thinner caused some momentary concern when he put it on. But Mrs. Hostetler was able to move the buttons over and achieve an approximate fit. A few days airing out got rid of the mothball smell. Waldo squeezed into the suit, loaded his prize pumpkin onto the pickup, and headed off on a long journey to the state fair.

The trip was quite an experience for a man who knew little of the world beyond his farm. The pumpkin was dutifully delivered and set in place for showing. Waldo spent the rest of the day walking around the fairway, marveling at the sights the likes of which he had never seen before. He was not ready yet for anything as daring as a ride on the Ferris wheel and his conscience kept him from attending any of the naughty sideshows. But he did get up nerve enough to pay five cents to throw some baseballs at milk bottles. He could almost feel himself getting more sophisticated by the minute. That night as he was falling asleep on the front seat of his pickup truck, he thought about the possibility of coming back to the fair in future years whether he had a prize pumpkin or not.

At the judging the next day there was really no contest. Waldo's pumpkin took first prize and instead of exploring the midway further, he stayed close to the pumpkin display to inform the visitors that he was the one who grew it. When one of the fair officials brought him an invitation to attend a dinner that evening with the rest of the prizewinners, Waldo was delighted. Here would be a chance to rub shoulders with the other winners, a very elite class.

"We'll have cocktails at 7:00 in the main administration building and dinner will be at 8:00," announced the fair official. "Everything will be free. It's our way of saying thanks to all of you who worked so hard to win blue ribbons."

Waldo took a whisk broom and brushed off his suit and headed for the administration building in plenty of time so that he wouldn't be late. He was hungry because in the excitement of the day he had forgotten to eat anything since breakfast. A free meal was exactly what he needed now. As he arrived at the administration building the crowd of winners was beginning to gather and make conversation. Several waiters with trays of cocktails were circulating among the people. One of the waiters stepped up to Waldo and asked him what he would like to have. Waldo looked at the tray of strange looking glasses, pointed to a cocktail and asked the waiter what that was. The waiter replied that it was a martini and an extra dry one at that. Even though it looked like a very small drink, Waldo took one because he had heard mention of a martini on a radio show once. The waiter's eyes got wider as Waldo took the martini in one swallow and put the glass on the tray.

"Would you like another?" the waiter asked sarcastically.

Waldo, being relatively unaware of nuances like sarcasm, said, "Thank you," and took another. He thought to himself, "Those things don't taste very good and they're not even as strong as the hard cider I make back at home."

The waiter, who now realized that he could have some sadistic fun with the naive farmer, made it a point to come back every few minutes to offer another martini. When the Master of Ceremonies rang the bell to signal the beginning of dinner, Waldo had consumed eight martinis in less than 45 minutes. He realized that he was starting to feel some strange effects, but he figured he would feel better when he got some food under his belt.

All of the guests sat down at the table and the announcer started to make some preliminary remarks before dinner. Suddenly Waldo realized that something was very wrong. The people across the table started to look blurry. His arms were so heavy he couldn't lift them off the table and it felt like all the blood was running to his feet.

He tried to remain cool as panic set in. He thought to himself, "Good Heavens. I'm having an attack. The only thing that will save me is if I get some food into my body right away."

The moderator was just completing his introduction of the man who was going to give the invocation. Suddenly Waldo called forth all of the energy he had left in his body and he managed to get his arms up off the table. He reached into the big salad bowl in front of him with both hands and started to stuff vegetables into his mouth. Then to the horror of all who were staring at him, Waldo picked up the pitcher of water and started to drink from it. Water splashed over his shoulders and ice cubes rolled down his back onto the floor. All of this was for naught because the final impact of the martinis was about to hit. Waldo started to shudder like he was beginning to have a fit. He stood upright, his eyes rolled back in his head, and he fell forward, unconscious, flat out on the table.

Needless to say, after Waldo was hauled out to the front seat of his pickup truck and those gathered were able to restore their composure, no other topic entered the conversation that evening. When the other diners realized that he was drunk and not sick and when they learned the number of martinis that he had consumed that evening, the laughter carried on into the night as the events were recounted over and over to the delight of all present.

The next day Waldo felt like a sledgehammer was pounding in his head. He managed to lift his prize pumpkin onto the back of the truck and he headed for home. He realized that he had been punished for his sinful ways and for letting pride overcome his good judgement. He also realized that the story of what happened at the Timonium fair would soon make its way back to the local community and any public appearance would surely be painful.

Waldo Hostetler continued to farm for many years and was active right up until the day he died and the farm passed on to his children. With every passing year he seemed to become even more reclusive. Time is usually forgiving when it comes to memories of bad experiences, but for a shy and sensitive man like Waldo, the embarrassing incident remained vivid in his mind. Those few people who were close enough to him to really know said he was never quite the same after the year that he raised the prize pumpkin.

The Woman with Two Husbands

It is still a mystery to me why the conservative people of the little town of Redland didn't make it a scandal of major proportions. A woman with two husbands at the same time was certainly not compatible with the religious teachings to which all of them subscribed. The Lutherans, the Methodists, and even the ultra-conservative Dunkers and Mennonites acted as though they didn't even notice the bizarre arrangement going on right under their noses. Mary Warren had two husbands, Mr. Warren and Alfred Wade, and all three lived under the same roof! The people of rural Maryland in the 1950's were swallowing a mortal sin and ignoring a chance for juicy gossip and a lawsuit without so much as a gentle complaint.

Their lack of attention was not because there was any attempt to hide the triangle. Mary and her two husbands participated in all the normal events husbands and wives did; it was just that instead of two people, there were three. They came to church and sat as a trio; the three went to town on Saturday and to the auction sales and the carnival in Rockville. It seemed weird even to us kids but if we ever asked anything about Mary and her husbands, we were quickly shushed. It was something nobody talked about. Even the most energetic gossips left it alone.

The Warrens, as they were known, lived five houses down from the crossroads. I remember walking or riding my bike by their house in the evening and seeing the three of them sitting on the front porch in rocking chairs. Mrs. Warren always sat in the middle. She was a tall, slender woman who still retained some of the modest beauty which was hers in her youth. She dressed conservatively, "matronly", in the vernacular of the day. She worked hard keeping house and caring for her two men. There were no children. Once when I asked my mother why there were no children she shushed me and my aunt said under her breath, "'Tis a blessing."

Mr. Warren and Mr. Wade had jobs which they drove to in separate cars each day. Mr. Warren worked locally as a carpenter; Mr. Wade had gotten a government job of some sort—probably maintenance work in Bethesda or Washington, D.C., large urban areas which were only a few miles away. Each evening they returned home and, in good weather, all three of them were working in the vegetable garden or on the front porch rocking by 7:00 P.M.

Whenever they went out in the car together, Mr. Warren and Mrs. Warren sat up front, with Mr. Wade in the back seat. One has to wonder how such arrangements came about, whether these were decisions arrived at through discussion and compromise or whether they occurred by accident. Whatever the source of the decision, the result seemed forever binding because they never deviated from their patterns of behavior.

Speculation abounded among us young people about their personal relationships. We weren't real sure of our facts because no sex education existed in those days in our area, but we knew enough to concoct theories about their sleeping habits. We would have given anything to know if all three slept in one bed. The small house appeared to have only one bedroom, but the specific sleeping arrangement was a mystery and still is to this day. No affection among the three was ever shown in public.

Much of the story of the woman with two husbands never became public. When I grew up and moved away from the area, the Warrens and Alfred Wade still maintained the intimate yet unusual relationship. The rule of no talk about their situation was maintained through some unwritten code which was not expressed. The otherwise strictly religious people ignored the indiscretion and admonished others for merely referring to it.

It was only recently that I learned the full story of the woman with two husbands. I returned to where I grew up to attend the funeral of an elderly, distant relative. I volunteered my car to transport several of the old people from the church to the cemetery and back to the church. Our route took us by the house where the Warrens had lived until their deaths.

It was then I decided to pep up the rather stilted conversation in my car by making a wisecrack. "From the wash on the line it looks like the woman who lives there now only has one husband at a time."

There was dead silence. I realized my attempt at humor was not appreciated by my passengers.

When we arrived at the church, I helped the three elderly people out of my car. First, a husband and wife who hobbled away without even a thank you. I knew I had trod on sacred ground. Then I took Mavis Jones' hand and supported her as she eased out of the car and stood upright. She held on to my hand and stared right into my eyes. I knew she was about to singe my tailfeathers.

She had known me all my life. She clerked at the country store where my family traded. Her motionless stare reminded me of the time she caught me collecting bottle deposits on nickel cola bottles I had taken off the back porch of the store.

"Boy, I think it's time you and me had a little talk. Take me up to my house." You never talked back to Mrs. Jones. I did exactly as she said.

The honeysuckle smelled sweet and the catbirds set up a howl as I took her arm and walked up to the brightly painted white benches under the maple trees in her backyard.

"You sit here a spell and I'll get us some sun tea."

I was uneasy. I didn't know why I had been summoned in this manner. Mavis Jones seemed friendly, but she had something on her mind, and I feared I was in for some straightening out. At age fifty-one I felt like a ten-year-old contemplating the wood shed.

She reappeared at the door and I hurried to help her carry the tea. She reluctantly accepted my assistance though I don't believe she could have managed on her own. She was feeble, a different person from the one I had known when I was growing up. She took a sip of tea, shaded her eyes from the bright sun with her hand, and then adjusted her position so she could look at me without the sun in her eyes. I waited to hear what she obviously meant to tell me.

"You were never a mean boy growing up, so I don't expect you are one now. Worst I can remember you doing is trying to cash in some pop bottles that weren't yours."

I was amazed but somehow not suprised that she remembered. "You said something about the Warrens today and you shouldn't have. You were trying to be funny but I guess you saw we didn't laugh." She was so right. My comment got stares of anger and this puzzled and embarrassed me.

"I'm going to tell you about the Warrens so you won't embarrass yourself again or slur the memory of three fine people."

The ice in my tea melted as the glass sat untouched and I listened spellbound to a story of love, loyalty, and understanding that surpassed anything I ever heard before. I also understood for the first time why the Warrens were never ostracized by the people of this little, conservative Maryland community.

Mrs. Warren had been married first to Alfred Wade. They had grown up in a neighboring community and were sweethearts in high school and some even said in junior high. Mary was a beautiful girl and Alfred a handsome boy; everyone said this was an ideal couple. Alfred starred on the baseball and basketball teams at a little community high school; Mary was a cheerleader and editor of the newspaper. In the yearbook it said they were both planning to go to college, a major ambition back in those days. But no one had planned for World War II which started in December of their senior year.

Mavis Jones interrupted her story long enough to greet a big black tomcat that had started rubbing back and forth on her leg. "Come here, precious. You're getting hungry, aren't you? You sit here with me now and we'll get you something in a few minutes." The cat curled up obediently in her lap.

I took a sip of my lukewarm tea and waited anxiously for the story to continue. Mavis stared up at the sky as she continued, as if some of the details required forced recollection.

She remembered that Mary and her high school sweetheart must have married in late May or early June of 1942 because she first met them that summer. Though the town in which they grew up was nearby, no one in Redland knew them until they moved into the small house that was rented to them by a relative who lived in Redland. They didn't get to live there long because Alfred went into the army that summer and Mary worked at various jobs a short while at the country store and then in a canning factory in a nearby town. It was there she met Mr. Warren, but as Mavis added with firmness designed to put aside any wrong ideas, she just knew him as a man, a fellow worker, who didn't go to war because he had flat feet.

"I will never forget the day that Mary got that awful telegram. It came just like any other letter except it told Mary her man was dead on some beach over in Italy. Lord, I've never seen anyone so broken up. We all tried to comfort her but it didn't do no good. I thought she'd cry herself to death.

"I learned that after a few weeks Mary went back to work to protect her sanity. She did all kinds of volunteer work, too, because it was so painful to be alone. Mary was young and attractive and after a while we advised her to be with other young people. But she wouldn't hear to it. She was still grieving real bad."

The people of Redland had just about given up on ever getting Mary interested in anyone after her beloved was killed in the war. Their surprise turned to delight when Mr. Warren started to call.

The ladies of the church tried to push the relationship along by inviting Mary and Mr. Warren to serve as co-chairpersons of various activities. It was obvious the blessing of the townspeople was upon the relationship of Mr. Warren and the Widow Wade.

The efforts were successful. After a reluctant start, Mary Wade started to welcome the interest of Mr. Warren. They actually began courting, and in a few months it was announced they would wed. It was a quiet ceremony befitting a widow and a second husband. There was no honeymoon. The week after they were married, they were occupying the house where Mary and Alfred had lived together so briefly.

Things settled down to a quiet routine and Redland turned its attention to other timely topics as World War II wore on. Blackouts provided the excitement many evenings as the little town practiced protecting itself against enemy attack, although it was never clear why anyone would bomb this little crossroads town.

Mavis Jones interrupted her story and asked if I needed more tea. I declined. She then went into the house and brought back some cream which she gave to the big tom cat which had been on her lap. When she settled back into the lawn chair, I sensed the climax of her story was about to unfold.

She really became serious as she related how, out of the blue, the War Department learned of the mistake. Alfred hadn't been killed. He was only a prisoner and now he was coming home to his wife. Mary was shocked into disbelief but it was true; her husband was returning home to her—and her new husband of two-and-a-half years.

No one knew what to do—not the preacher, not the county judge, not anybody. There was no precedent. What should Mary do? Was she now Mrs. Warren or Mrs. Wade?

Country people show a logic that is often misunderstood by more sophisticated people. Maybe there should have been a legal decision. Maybe the church should have ruled. Neither did because Mary Wade-Warren made a decision. She had committed to both men in good faith. If they could live with the reality so could she. And so could the people of Redland who saw this as an act of God, a situation which no one could have foreseen or prevented. The people respected Mary's decision to live with two men, the husbands apparently saw the logic, and the matter was put to rest.

Mavis Jones ended her story but didn't wait for my reaction. Her reasoning was not on trial. Rather, it was my opportunity for enlightenment. She picked up my glass which signaled that I was dismissed. I started to walk to my car and she took hold of my arm.

"They were good people who were caught in the middle of a terrible war. Who were we to judge them?"

Who indeed! I walked back to my car and started toward the interstate. Something caused me to pause. I headed back to the Lutheran cemetery where we had been earlier that day. I walked to the Warren plot and looked at the headstones. There

I saw a marble marker with writing the likes of which I had never seen before. The headstone said:

> Kenneth Warren, Mary Warren, Alfred Wade
> Beloved Wife and Husbands

There was also this inscription on the headstone:

> We are not given to understand
> but put our faith in one
> whose wisdom can make all things straight.

Somehow it all made sense.

A Forgotten Letter

Annie grew up a child without roots. Her parents died when she was eight years old and from then on she was shuttled among well-meaning relatives who wanted to do their share but who never really made her a part of the family. Each year meant a different school in a different community. Friendships could never be looked upon as long-term relationships, so she became withdrawn to decrease the inevitable pain of parting.

Summers were worst of all because they were always spent with Aunt Maureen, a maiden lady who lived in the city. Apparently, the relatives had decided collectively that Aunt Maureen's cultured ways were essential for a young girl growing up. No doubt all involved in the decision meant well, but too many years separated the old woman and the young girl.

The neighborhood of row houses where Aunt Maureen lived had once been elegant but now seemed part of a Currier and Ives past which had surrendered to suburbia. Most people who lived there were old folks, too poor to move but fearful of encroaching decline which would inevitably make this part of town a slum. Only Annie's passive ways made it possible for her to exist behind a front door with four bolt locks and iron-barred windows.

Aunt Maureen was not unkind, but she knew nothing about children. She was struggling with her own feelings about aging and confused by the rapid changes in her world. She required

Annie to dress like a proper lady, even during brief forays into the tiny front yard. Infrequent trips to the store on the corner called for a hat and gloves. Mealtimes were quiet affairs where reminders about posture and manners were the mainstay of conversation.

The summer of Annie's thirteenth year brought a surprising and exciting change. The old man who lived alone next door died and a retired couple, the Breadys, bought the home. They had never had children of their own, but they were both retired teachers who had worked a lifetime with children. Annie became their project and, in return, the Breadys became her escape from Aunt Maureen and her stuffy ways.

Aunt Maureen didn't mind the fact that Annie spent most of her time next door. After all, the Breadys were teachers, so how could this be harmful? In truth, Maureen was relieved to be free of the responsibility. The mandatory return for meals was suspended more and more frequently; this meant Annie didn't have to stuff down a second dinner to salve Aunt Maureen's conscience. By the second and third summers, just about all the days were spent with the Breadys, and Aunt Maureen's house was for sleeping only.

The Breadys were exciting people, in love with life and always active. Their house was filled with books and they talked about the world and what was happening. They took Annie with them on expeditions to the library and museum. They convinced her that she was bright and they taught her the possibilities of life. Annie saved up her report cards each year to show the Breadys at the beginning of summer. They praised her as her grades improved from year to year. They listened as she worked through, in her own mind, the normal problems of growing up.

There was no special ceremony at the end of Annie's sixteenth summer. Perhaps it was because neither she nor the Breadys realized that this was the last summer they would be together. Next year was the end of high school and the start of the job which made college possible—an aspiration culminated in the previous summer from a dream forged gradually as her confidence grew from year to year.

Annie continued to grow and finished college and was in law school when she heard of Mrs. Bready's death. She had kept in touch, nominally at least, by sending the obligatory cards on holiday occasions. Lord knows she loved them enough, but time just slipped away. The letters and cards became less frequent and the quality of contact less personal. She cared but there was so little time in such a busy schedule of a successful young woman. She just couldn't go to the funeral when Mrs. Bready died; the spray of flowers was the best she could do.

She was comforted some by the fact that she had taken time to write a special letter to them in her senior year of college. It was one of those things that just comes over you. She was daydreaming during a respite from study—thinking about those beautiful summers of her youth and growth. It seemed like the right thing to do. She wrote a letter to the Breadys telling them how much they had meant to her.

"It is because of you that I am in college and plan to go on to law school. You cared for me when I had doubts about myself. You showed me how wonderful life can be in spite of my lack of family. You became my family and for that I can never repay you. I love you with all my heart." No reply to the letter was ever received but none was expected. It wasn't the kind of letter that called for an answer.

Going to Mr. Bready's funeral was not at all convenient but Annie felt she must. This was the last opportunity to pay respects and, though the temptation of making an excuse was strong, schedules were juggled to permit the trip. She was glad she went because there were so few in attendance. Without the usual number of children and grandchildren at such an event there are few to attend the funeral of an old person.

At the graveside there were only the preacher, the undertaker, Annie, and Carl Boggs, the family lawyer. After a brief ceremony the preacher paused and nodded to Mr. Boggs who stepped forward with some papers in his hands.

"Since the Breadys have no living relatives, they have directed me to take care of some final details. All of their worldly goods are to be sold and the proceeds given to the college they attended. Additionally, there are these items which they called treasures beyond monetary value which they wanted buried with whichever was the last to die. These items have meaning only to them so it is fitting that they not be scattered about."

The undertaker opened the casket for a moment while Mr. Boggs deposited, with gentle reverence, two college diplomas, a marriage license, and a much-worn letter from a young girl in her senior year of college.

The Hunter

Hal Morris awoke before the motel operator even made the wake-up call. The linoleum floor was cold to his bare feet as he made his way to the tiny bathroom which consisted of a toilet, a basin, and a metal shower stall. It was a modest lodging place at the foot of a ridge of mountains, a motel that made most all of its money during the deer-hunting season. Hunters stopped there only briefly on their way to the hunt since the location made it possible to get a night's sleep and still be in the deer blind before daylight.

"That electric heater does a pretty good job of keeping everything warm but the floor," he thought to himself. "I'd sure like to have one up in the blind because it will be colder than a well-digger's boots up there."

Hal went to the motel office to get his thermos filled with coffee, then wiped the frost from the windshield of his car and started up the mountain the few miles to where the road ended.

"There ought to be good hunting up here since the government opened up this area to hunters," he thought. "At least there better be good hunting, as much as I paid to lease this blind."

The frozen grass crunched under his feet as he followed the flashlight beam along the path. The freezing chill was made even more biting to his nose and lips by the slight breeze that became more evident the higher up the mountain he walked.

"At least that deer blind will cut down on the wind," he mused aloud, "but it will still be cold up here. It will be worth it when I get my deer."

Hal knew he was kidding himself when he tried to justify hunting based on economics. The cost of the lease and all of the paraphernalia necessary for the hunt far exceeded the value of the meat he would get. No, the reason for the hunt was something else. Killing an animal renewed his feeling of masculinity and gave him bragging rights with his peers. It may have even made up for some of the insecurity in the rest of his life.

The deer blind was a wooden structure big enough for two people. It looked like an old-fashioned outhouse with a door in the back and a small window in front for a gun portal. One hundred yards ahead was a grassy clearing in the trees. In the center of the clearing was a feeder which the lease owner kept filled with corn. The feeder had a battery-powered timer which caused corn to be released every morning and evening. During the months prior to hunting season the deer were trained to feed on the corn in the clearing. They became so tame that even the noise of the feeder discharging corn no longer alarmed them. The deer would come, wait for the free meal, and then graze leisurely in the clearing. It also made it easy to kill the trusting deer from the blind so close to the clearing.

This practice of tricking these gentle animals gave Hal some feelings of guilt, but it was legal and, after all, it virtually assured getting a deer. The high-powered telescope-equipped rifle at close range made it possible to even pick the spot on the animal for the bullet to enter so that good cuts of meat wouldn't be spoiled. Hal rationalized the great edge he had over the simple beast by trying to place his shot right in the brain.

"This way there is really no pain felt. Besides, these animals need to be harvested or they will get too numerous and overpopulate the land," he said to himself.

The darkness started to turn to gray as dawn approached. Hal had his high-powered rifle resting on the frame of the gun portal ready to aim. He didn't have to wait long before several deer emerged from the woods, waiting for their free meal. Hal aimed at one and then another, trying to decide which one to kill. He had a choice of bucks, does, and fawns of various ages and sizes.

There was a twinge of uneasiness as Hal prepared to play the role of executioner. The crosshairs in his rifle sight moved from a large buck to a fawn to a doe about three years old. "That doe is the one I want," he thought. "She won't be too heavy to carry back to the car and her meat should be tender. And killing a young deer will do more to control the population than killing an old one."

He placed the crosshairs right in front of the deer's left ear and gently squeezed the trigger of the rifle. The loud report startled the other deer and they bolted into the woods. The bullet pierced the skull of the doe, making a small hole where it entered but nearly tearing away half of the skull as it exited. He didn't hurry to the clearing because he knew he had made a clean kill.

Hal dragged the deer to the edge of the clearing and prepared to field-clean the carcass. Taking his knife out of its shield, he pierced the doe's neck to drain out the blood. The crimson fluid melted the ice crystals on the grass as it fell to the ground. "This is the part of hunting I don't like. Cleaning the carcass is grisly business."

He then slit the young female from her neck to the base of her tail. He shoved his gloved hand between the ribs, grabbed the intestines, and pulled the entrails out of the carcass for buzzards to eat later. His hand felt warm as he wrenched the organs from the body and flung them to the ground. He wiped his bloody hands on his trousers and lifted the carcass to his shoulders for the walk back to the car. He laid the deer across the car's hood and tied the legs to the fender. The half-remaining head dangled with the tongue stretched forward as if the creature had been garroted.

Hal stopped where the sign said "Deer Cleaned and Frozen."

"You weren't after a trophy this time, I take it?" the man said as he pondered the carcass.

"No," Hal replied. "I was after tender meat. I've got racks of antlers at home already."

The next stop was the car wash where the blood was cleaned from the car. Hal washed his hands and even sprayed his trousers with the hose. He wanted to rid himself of the blood as quickly as possible.

Once at home, he changed clothes and showered, then joined his wife and ten-year-old son at the lunch table. He proceeded to tell the story of his conquest, embellishing his performance and diminishing the role of electric deer-feeders, high-powered rifles, and deer blinds. The size of the deer grew larger, the distance of the shot farther, as all the details were shifted to Hal's favor. The story caused Hal's son to be overcome with excitement and he asked when he would finally be allowed to join in a hunt.

Hal was pleased that his son wanted to go, and responded to the question immediately. "How would you like to go with me next weekend?" The boy was ecstatic but his mother was reluctant.

"You keep telling me of the dangers, how those men go up there to get drunk more than hunt and how they shoot at anything that moves," complained Mrs. Morris. "Sometimes they are too drunk to shoot straight so they only wound the poor creatures who go off to bleed or starve to death. What kind of thing is that for a ten-year-old to see?"

The boy's pleadings outweighed all objections. Friday night of the next week, Hal and his son were off on their first hunt together. They drove to the motel at the foot of the mountain and checked in. Every detail of the trip was carefully explained by the father to a wide-eyed and receptive son.

The clerk at the hotel said they could have most any room in the place, a very unusual situation near a holiday period. "Them crazies done scared everybody away," explained the clerk. "They even shot at some of the hunters' cars and winged one fella in a blind."

He was talking about a family that lived on the mountain. Prior to the opening of the area for hunting, this family had it pretty much to themselves. They didn't consider their hunting illegal because they hunted only for food, not sport. The mountain men were so angry at the intrusion of other hunters that they were threatening to kill anyone who appeared.

"Hunters have been canceling their reservations. Glad you two didn't," said the clerk.

Hal had not heard about the problem and surely would not have brought his son if he had. "What are the game wardens doing to secure the area?" asked Hal.

The clerk replied that they were out in force this weekend. This was all the reassurance Hal needed. "If the wardens are out in force, you can bet those hillbillies have hightailed it out of the county by now," he said.

He and his son went off to their room to get some sleep before the 4:30 rising time. The excitement of anticipation soon gave way to fatigue from the trip and both were soon soundly asleep.

It seemed only a short time since Hal had fallen asleep when the night silence was broken by a shotgun blast. Hal sat upright in his bed. Just as he reached for the light switch, the lock on the door was smashed by the heel of a hunter's boot. Hal found himself peering into the muzzle of a double-barreled shotgun pointed right at his face.

"Make a move and go to glory without your head," said the bearded mountain man. "You came a huntin' and you became the game. Now ain't that a shame."

"Wait, I'll give you anything we have," pleaded Hal. By this time his son had been awakened by the noise and was staring, petrified with fear at the sight of the rough mountain man pointing the gun at his father.

"Please, I'll do anything you say, but don't harm us," Hal begged.

"You come up here and kill our deer just for fun. You don't even need food. I'm goin' to stop you right here. There will be two less to worry about," the old man said with a grin.

"Why kill us? We'll leave and, believe me, we'll never come back," Hal begged.

"There's too many of you. You are spreading out all over the place. I've got to thin your numbers. If somebody doesn't, you'll soon take over this place," replied the old man.

Hal became brave out of desperation and asked that his son be released and that he alone be killed. His pleading used every ounce of his energy as he begged for mercy, sweat beading on his face, tears in his eyes. "Please! Spare the boy!"

"No, I think I better kill him first," replied the man. "You're old and won't be hunting much longer. That young 'un needs to be killed first, cause he could be trouble for a long time."

With that the mountain man placed the muzzle of the gun against the terrified boy's forehead. He grinned a sickly grin and slowly squeezed the trigger of the double-barreled shotgun.

Hal bolted upright in bed, his heart beating rapidly. He reached for the light and muttered, "Thank God!" as he saw his son sleeping peacefully at his side.

"What a nightmare! It was so damn real I could smell the powder from that gun. Thank God, thank God, it was only a dream."

The young boy couldn't understand why they stayed such a very short time in the deer blind that morning and why his dad never saw a deer worth shooting. He couldn't understand what caused his father's sudden loss of enthusiasm. He never learned of the dream.

His father never took him hunting again, nor did he go himself. He turned down every invitation by giving some excuse. He even sold his gun collection, said hunting wasn't worth the trouble. It had cost too much and, besides, it no longer presented a sufficient challenge.

The Estate Sale

In rural America such events are a mixture of sadness and joyful anticipation. An estate sale means someone has died or become too feeble for self maintenance; this can be very sad. But for those looking for a bargain, especially those unacquainted with the dispossessed, there is potential happiness like that which comes from finding a thing of value in the public domain.

Rosemary Carnes had few things of value and quite a few friends, so this sale seemed destined to be a sad occasion. Her children did not have the wherewithal to support her, so in keeping with state law, all her worldly goods were to be sold at public auction to the highest bidder to defray the cost of her care in a public nursing home.

The professional auctioneer, who was also a real estate salesman and notary public, brought his staff to Rosemary's home to prepare the goods for sale. These part-time workers had become callous from doing this frequently over the years. Nonetheless, they always had the feeling of being an interloper in someone's private quarters. One woman, emptying a drawer of bedclothes which had been carefully stored, said she felt like she was peeking into a bedroom.

"No sooner did Mr. Carnes die than they cart his wife off to a nursing home and then sell her private things. It just don't seem right. I wish I didn't need the few dollars I get to pull all this stuff out for the sale."

The furniture and other household goods were spread out on the lawn for the sale which would begin at noon. The ladies from the church were busy preparing lemonade and sandwiches. It was a rather humble collection of items for sale, characteristic of furnishings acquired in the Depression years of the 1930's. The furniture was rough and solid—functional, but not ornate in any way. Much of it was homemade rather than purchased from a furniture store.

One piece stood out in glaring contrast to all the rest. In the midst of the solid oak furniture there was a delicate Queen Anne sofa made of cherry wood. The auctioneer knew it was of special value and planned his strategy accordingly. If it didn't bring at least $200, he had his "buy-in" man ready to top the real bid and hold the item for private sale. The unsuspecting public never knew that a buy-in man was there to artificially bid prices up to insure a minimum price on selected items. The auctioneer worked on a percentage basis, so the buy-in man he provided was valuable to the person holding the auction as well as to the auctioneer.

The auction moved ahead in a predictably routine manner.

Items sold at a bargain but not much below real worth. The buy-in man saw to that. The auctioneer saved the Queen Anne sofa until the last. The bidding started high because several people, including furniture dealers, sensed its worth. Once the bidding passed the $300 point, the buy-in man quit bidding, but others carried it on to $500, then $600, and the eyes of the spectators grew larger. The bidding between two furniture dealers reached $1,450. From there the auctioneer urged them up fifty dollars at a time. The bid reached $1,640 and the low bidder turned and walked away. The high bidder smiled a nervous smile, wondering whether he had gone too high. The auctioneer said, "Going once, going twice."

Just then a handsome figure of a man stepped forward. His graying hair revealed his years, but his straight posture and bearing showed breeding. To the shock and amazement of all assembled, he bid $2,000. No one was game to challenge the bid. The auctioneer cried "Sold!" and the Queen Anne sofa was committed to the stranger who quickly called forth his men to take immediate possession and load the sofa onto a truck. While the crowd gazed in awe, the stranger paid cash, and then he and his men boarded their vehicles and were gone.

A buzz ran through the crowd as they speculated upon this unexpected turn of events. All sorts of stories justifying the special worth of the Queen Anne sofa and the identity of the mystery man surfaced in the coming days and weeks. Everything from treasure hidden in the frame to a special love experience on its surface were offered explanations. No one ever found out for sure, though they could have if Reverend Sanders had told the story only he knew. The mystery of the handsome man who outbid all challengers and acquired the beautiful Queen Anne sofa still provides speculation to this day.

Rosemary Carnes grew up in a wealthy family in this small town. The years prior to World War I were years of prosperity, particularly for the few wealthy families who lived there. The area around the town was worked by less wealthy farmers who share-cropped the land. Rosemary met a boy of her own breeding, Albert Hartshorn, and they fell in love. It was an idyllic courtship until the economic crash of 1929 which ended their plans for marriage and resulted in their separation. The wealthy people lost their land. Albert moved away. Rosemary was forced into a marriage of economic convenience with John Carnes, a good man from the working class. Rosemary tried to love John, but her heart was with Albert, though she never saw him again. Rosemary endured her working life as a farm wife, pretended in her contacts with John, but never really fooled herself or him. She and her husband plodded through life, working at their commitments and on the edge of happiness. Polite to each other, pleasant and supportive, but never in love.

Each year on the small farm was a struggle filled with uncertainty. Some years crops failed and debts built up. Others were better and farmers almost broke even; never was there a surplus or profit. Only one year was different. The rains fell at just the right times and the harvest was a record. John kissed Rosemary as he left for the city to sell the grain. It was a happy day because at last they would be getting ahead.

Rosemary waited late that night for John's return. She had prepared a celebration, his favorite meal and sherry wine, treasured for years, the gift of a friend. She waited far beyond the time when John should have returned. Her emotions were mixed of anger and fear.

John returned just before midnight but in a most uncustomary condition for such a hard working, predictable man. Too drunk to be driving the truck but, by luck, safe, John staggered in and hugged his amazed Rosemary. Her relief turned to shock when she learned that John had spent most of the money from the sale of grain to buy her a present.

"I've never been good enough for you and I've never given you the things you deserve. This may be the last chance I ever have to give you a present worthy of such a fine woman."

Rosemary's feelings were bittersweet as John uncovered a beautiful Queen Anne sofa, the likes of which she had not seen since the years of her youth. It was hard to be angry at such a gesture, even though it meant a return to the struggle of making financial ends meet rather than enjoying a period of being financially ahead.

Not much was said about the couch after that, but it became the center of Rosemary's existence and her contact with her past. Important visitors were invited to sit on it. Rosemary occasionally sat there to read, but otherwise it was preserved with a heavy cover. No other family members ever used it. No such rule was ever stated; it was just understood.

Life on the farm continued much as it had in former years—a constant struggle for survival. The children left home to start their own struggles for survival. John and Rosemary worked even harder without the help of the children until the work was finally too much for them to manage. John was trying to sell the farm to get enough money for a modest retirement when he died suddenly.

Friends advised Rosemary to take the state's offer of a nursing home for life in return for her farm. It was a hard thing for her to accept, but eventually she did—in reality there was little choice.

Reverend Sanders helped the aging woman through the transition and it was during one of these counseling sessions that he learned how the Queen Anne sofa had been acquired. He had often wondered how this out-of-place piece of furniture came into the possession of the poor farm people. He also learned why it was precious to Rosemary. It was not only her contact with a prosperous past, but it was her reminder of the time when she planned to marry Albert Hartshorn—a love which had never cooled even though it had been torn from her grasp by circumstances beyond anyone's control. Reverend Sanders learned that she loved Albert as much today as when they were carefree sweethearts, though she had not seen him in forty years.

Rosemary never knew of Reverend Sanders' successful efforts to locate Albert Hartshorn or the fact that they talked about her and her undying love. Albert's life had returned him to prosperity and given him a loyal wife and loving family, but he, too, never overcame his first real love. It was only Reverend Sanders who knew who the distinguished gentleman was who paid such an outrageous price for the Queen Anne sofa, and it was only he who knew that the sofa was to be delivered anonymously to Rosemary at the nursing home.

A Teacher's Decision

Mr. Talbot felt his hand begin to tremble as he read the letter from John Wellman, a boy he had taught in high school twenty years before. The intervening years of teaching and five years of retirement had not dulled his recollection of the incident. It was the one and only time Mr. Talbot had deviated from his tough, no nonsense standards. His credo "You get what you earn, no more, no less" was a trademark which he wore with pride. Only this one time had he violated his own rule. The letter brought back to his mind that decision and it added a disturbing twist.

Mr. Talbot was an experienced math teacher when the situation occurred and, even though he had seniority, he still had to teach one class of dummy math. This was the term given to a fundamentals of math course for students who had to have one math credit to graduate. A "D" in this course meant a student could graduate. Failure meant the whole course had to be repeated next year or in summer school. Those who failed usually dropped out of school and never received a diploma.

Talbot had little compassion for these students because most had enough ability to do well, but instead they were lazy and lacked any semblance of ambition.

John Wellman was typical of the students in the class: a clown, smart aleck, and loafer. When his final exam came out to a sixty-nine and a half points Talbot quickly placed an "F" on the top of the paper. There was even a good feeling of justice done, maybe even retribution, in Mr. Talbot's mind as Johnny Wellman got just what he deserved. Besides, Johnny's parents had tried to influence a grade in an earlier marking period. This would show them!

But there was a complicating factor. Vernon Jones got a sixty-nine and a half, too. Vernon was not typical of the class. Instead, he used every bit of his limited ability, always applied himself, showed respect for authority and was a perfect gentleman. Vernon Jones needed to graduate because his parents were poor and they needed him to work in their store. Each time Mr. Talbot was in the store, Vernon's parents expressed gratitude for all he had done for their son.

Mr. Talbot was in a dilemma. Though he was, by nature, inclined to give no one a break under any conditions, this case seemed unusually deserving. "If I give Vernon a "D", I'll have to do the same for Johnny Wellman. They are the only two borderline scores. Those Wellman parents will have me in court if they find I gave a "D" to one and not to the other.

His compassion for Vernon Jones was overwhelming. Mr. Talbot placed a "D" at the top of his paper and then sifted back through the tests until he found Johnny's paper, drew a line through the "F", and placed a "D" beside it. As expected, Vernon and his parents went out of their way to express appreciation. And, also as expected, he never heard from Johnny Wellman or his parents.

Now, twenty years later, Mr. Talbot had a letter from John Wellman. He reread it slowly, pausing to reflect on his decision so many years before.

Dear Mr. Talbot,
  I have started to write this letter many times to thank you for the special consideration you showed in high

school when you gave me a passing grade I did not deserve. I know how you feel about standards, so the message had a powerful impact when I saw you had marked through the "F", which I had earned, and you gave me a "D" instead. I must admit I pondered for a while over this surprising action on your part, but as time passed I understood your message. You were saying that you had faith in me in spite of my immaturity. I felt you were giving me a final chance to make something of my life.

All that summer I agonized over what I should do. I really hadn't expected to graduate. With the diploma you made possible I had new options and, frankly, a new obligation. I could no longer dismiss college on the grounds that I had not graduated. When I made a casual visit to the junior college I found people there like you—people who believed in second chances for boys with ability who wanted to change. They admitted me and I'm pleased to report that my grades at the end of two years were good enough to get me into university and then on to law school.

In my practice of law and in my civic work, I am trying to pay back to the world a debt that is due in large measure to you. You didn't give up on me and you caused me to see in myself positive things I hadn't seen before.

My prayer is that you will enjoy many years of health and happiness in your retirement.

> Respectfully yours,
> John Wellman, J.D.

Mr. Talbot dropped his hand with the letter to his lap and stared thoughtfully out the window. He tried to recall how many other students there had been who ended the course with a sixty-nine and a half average.

Guilty by Appearance

Even at 9:00 A.M. it was oppressively hot in the little southern Maryland town. July was like that but it didn't stop the crowd of townspeople who wanted to see the trial. It was the best show in town, far superior to the cheap movie which was shown on weekends at the theater. Eaton was the county seat in a very poor rural county, so a visiting judge and a jury trial constituted an event of outstanding proportions in 1938.

This trial provided even greater appeal. Because of the people involved, it was sure to be standing room only, even in the old, sultry, humid courtroom. Mather Williams, a black man, was on trial for grand theft. An eyewitness swore he saw Mather leaving the scene of a burglary of the largest grocery store in town. Even though Mather was a church-going family man, everyone knew he had been doing poorly in his trucking business and that one of his trucks had been repossessed by the finance company. The kind of things stolen—fresh meats, cases of canned goods—were probably the things he needed for his large family.

The lawyer defending Mather added the final dramatic touch to the trial. Milt Calvin was a local hero. Mr. Everything while in high school, he had gone off to the state university to study law. This was his first case after returning home. Some people said he'd be smart enough to plead Mather guilty and seek the mercy of the visiting judge. Others said he had too much pride for that. Most people felt Mather was guilty but Milt would probably put on a defense anyway, because that was the way he had always been. Milt was a fighter on the football field so he would probably fight here, too, even though it was a losing cause.

The courtroom was filled to overflowing that morning with sweltering citizens who tried to keep themselves cool with fans from the local funeral parlor. It was 8:45 and time for the combatants to enter the arena. The district attorney entered and acknowledged several of his friends who had gotten in line early and acquired prized seats. Mather was brought in, wearing street clothes rather than the county jail uniform, but he was in shackles. Spectators stretched their necks to see when young Calvin would enter to face his first test in the real world of the criminal justice system. Even the most veteran of the trial attenders was not prepared for what they saw.

The audience stared in disbelief as Milton Calvin entered from the rear, down the center aisle, to take his place beside his client. His hair was uncombed, he had a three-day beard, and he wore dungarees and a crumpled shirt with no tie. The hush of the crowd gave way to whispered conversation as everybody tried to figure what was going on.

Some conjectured that he had been on a drunk, others that the university had scrambled his brains with that new book-learning. All were sure of one thing: when that old judge gets here he will throw this lawyer in jail for sure.

The bailiff gave the order, "All rise," and the gray-haired judge entered and took his seat. In seconds his eyes fell upon Milt Calvin and he ordered him to approach the bench. The courtroom fell silent as an obviously angered judge conversed with young Calvin in hushed tones. To the surprise of everyone, the judge did not jail Milton or even hold him in contempt. Instead, he let him return to his client and the trial proceeded.

In spite of the continued distraction of Milton's dress, the routine of the trial moved swiftly. The jury was selected and the district attorney put on his case. The eyewitness said it was a Negro man he saw and identified Mather. Milton Calvin pressed him on cross-examination, pointing out that the distance was too great for positive identification, among many other things. The witness held firm.

In any other state, the evidence would have been too weak for even an indictment, but this was Maryland in the 1930's. The guilt of a black man on trial was a forgone conclusion and the trial a very easy task for the prosecutor. The only suspense usually came in the length of the sentence. The odds this day, discussed in the diner across from the courthouse during lunch, favored one year to three, with three the most likely since Milton Calvin had offended the judge. Many shook their heads in sympathy at the dumb thing Milton had done to poor Mather.

By 3:00 the trial was over except the summation by the lawyers before the jury voted. The district attorney gave an impassioned speech about how nobody is safe from thieves these days and how people could sleep easier with Mather in jail. The white audience in the courtroom nodded in agreement. The black people in the Jim Crow balcony stared stoically as they heard these familiar words. Then it was the defense attorney's turn to address the jury.

Milton pointed out the fine, church-going reputation of Mather Williams. This made little impact on the assembled crowd or the jury. Speeches like that were usually designed to lighten the sentence, nothing else. He then reviewed the weak circumstantial evidence, but little would come of that because evidence played a minor role in trials where prejudice is the real issue. Milton Calvin knew that, so he went to the heart of the issue.

"Your Honor, I am indisposed. May I have a ten-minute recess before I conclude my presentation to the jury?"

The judge agreed but no one left the courtroom because they knew ten minutes meant exactly ten minutes. The spectators just shook their heads at another obvious irregularity by this inexperienced lawyer.

In exactly ten minutes, the bailiff said, "All rise." The judge entered and at the same time Milton Calvin entered. The audience was amazed at the change in Milton. He was dressed in a navy blue, pin-striped suit with a maroon tie. He was shaven, combed, and a perfect example of tasteful dress.

"Ladies and gentlemen, I ask you to reflect for a moment. What did you think of me when I appeared to defend this man? Did you think I was a poor lawyer because of my offensive dress? Then I ask you, did I not perform well as a lawyer? You may have even been surprised that I knew the law even though I was dressed like a vagrant.

"Members of the jury, I am the same man. If outward appearances caused you to pre-judge me, then the term for that is 'prejudice.' Bear in mind, I can change my clothes. Mather cannot change the color of his skin. If any of you are planning to vote guilty, I ask you if your decision is based on the evidence or the color of the defendant's skin."

Milton thanked the judge for allowing him to make his point. The jury deliberated a very short while, which surprised nobody who had witnessed the trial. Neither was there any surprise at the verdict of "Not Guilty."

E. McKinley Smythe

Anyone who knew him when he was growing up called him
Eddy Smith. But the sign on the small house that doubled as
a mortuary said "E. McKinley Smythe—Mortician and Undertaker." Eddy felt the high-sounding name more in keeping with
his profession and more commercially acceptable. No one
would want to be buried by the Eddy Smith Funeral Home.

In spite of his modest surroundings, Eddy was a good undertaker. He had apprenticed under a fine make-up man in a large
mortuary in the city and he learned his lessons well. He could
take a body disfigured in a fire or accident and patch it up for
a reasonable viewing. He could put smiles on people whose
smiling muscles had long since atrophied. He was a skilled
technician, as good as any around. His modest funeral parlor
and lack of business were not a true testimony to his skill.

Eddy had a problem: his weakness for alcohol prevented real
success. Everybody in the small town knew about it so he was
destined to bury only paupers and pensioners, rather than the
folks from the big church in town, the First Baptist Church. The
burying of poor people and a small ambulance service kept him
afloat. His hearse became an ambulance when he simply
changed the sign in the window. People who knew better refused
to be transported in an ambulance that doubled as a hearse.

Then one day the E. McKinley Smythe Funeral Home got
its big chance. The undertaker in town had two funerals on

the same day and a third death overtaxed their capabilities. Reluctantly, the third family engaged E. McKinley Smythe's Funeral Home to perform the needed services for a deceased widow lady.

Eddy was thrilled. He had a chance for a big breakthrough. He shined the hearse and made sure all of the equipment for lowering the casket was in good repair. He didn't want any squeaking pulleys to take away from the solemnness of the occasion. He did a make-up job on the old lady that amazed even her closest kin. She looked twenty years younger and a lot more alive than she had for years.

The day of the funeral was a crucial one for Eddy. If he was to break into the big time there could be no hitch. He got his handyman to help him load the body into the hearse for the trip to the church. Everything was going according to plan, except Eddy needed a drink.

He had rewarded himself for getting this prestigious assignment by buying a bottle of the most expensive scotch, not the cheap stuff he normally drank. He had planned to wait until after the funeral to sample it but the excitement was too much. He decided to take the bottle along for occasional discreet sips, large enough to boost courage but small enough not to impair discretion. He took one sip out of the quart bottle, relished the thought of the many sips ahead, then hid the bottle in the hearse in a spray of flowers.

Arriving at the church, he was surprised to find the pastor and pallbearers waiting to meet the hearse. Eddy had thought there would be time to take a nip and stash the bottle while placing the flowers in the church. Now he had to act fast so that his bottle would not be discovered. He plopped a Sen-Sen in his mouth, greeted the pastor, and excused himself to make a few adjustments before the flowers and casket could be taken into the church.

He could not put the bottle in the glove compartment as planned because he would be seen and he couldn't leave it in the flowers. There was no other choice. He had to put it in the casket at the feet of the deceased where it couldn't be seen during the viewing of the body.

All through the service Eddy thought only of his precious bottle of expensive scotch. While others were praying for the departed soul, he was praying for the return of his bottle. Perhaps he could retrieve it during the trip from the church to the cemetery.

Some of the eulogy seemed strangely fitting to a progressively desperate Eddy. "Dear friends and loved ones," the reverend intoned. "Do not think of this as a loss but as a gain for heaven." For just a moment Eddy pictured his beloved bottle being carried to heaven by the widow, and Saint Peter sipping whiskey the likes of which he had never experienced in Bible times. "The memory of the departed will be with us as long as we may live." Eddy agreed with that. It was the best whiskey he had ever tasted and he remembered it well. "We the living must resolve to suffer this loss and go on with gratitude for having known her for this brief time." This was too much to ask of Eddy.

"I've got to get that bottle out of that casket," he was thinking.

His plan was thwarted by the reverend who decided to ride to the cemetery in the hearse. The widow and the bottle were lowered into the grave as tears flowed from a small group of bereaved family and friends. The tears also flowed freely from the attending undertaker, a sight not commonly seen by the good members of the First Baptist Church.

So touched were the mourners with Eddy's emotional response that they soon spread the word. Eddy's obvious dedication to his profession and his genuine concern for the departed caught the people's attention. No one could remember any undertaker who cried as much or more than the deceased's own family!

Within weeks the E. McKinley Smythe Funeral Parlor became the official undertaking establishment for the whole town, including the First Baptist Church. Eddy enjoyed success in keeping with his abilities but was careful to reward himself more discreetly, lest his good fortune be jeopardized. His crying at graveside became an expected touch which he found simple and easy to continue. When tears were needed he simply recalled that day when the bottle of prize scotch went six feet under to stay.

The Last Public Hanging in the County

It didn't seem possible that forty-seven years had passed since that day which etched itself forever in my mind. It was a puzzling, confusing day, full of excitement and mystery for a six-year-old who was to witness the last public hanging in this small Maryland town. It wasn't intended for me to witness this event; my father just happened to come in from the farm for coffee and probably some beer. I had learned that trips to town often meant that. I loved to be with my dad and he had given in to my pleas to tag along. This just happened to be the day for the hanging.

The huge elm tree is still there and you can even see where the ropes burned the limb as many bodies "danced four feet off the ground" over the years. The statue of a Confederate officer still stares off toward the South, his back defiantly turned toward the Yankee North. The old courthouse is there, but it is now used as a warehouse.

The grass seems much greener than before because there are few people treading across the lawns. People have moved to the suburbs, and this part of the old town seems more like a museum or something out of a time warp. As I sit on the park bench looking at the Hanging Tree, I wonder if any of these people living here know what the town was like in the old days. There are a quarter million people living here now. There were twelve hundred then. The streets were narrow, the parking lots unpaved, and there were no malls or supermarkets. This was the center of activity, as well as the town center geographically.

Our 1931 Chevrolet chugged into the parking lot by the feed store and my father pulled the big lever which set the parking brake. The red clay of the parking lot was covered with cinders which settled out of the smoke of the many passing steam trains. People in railroad towns were used to soot being a part of everything they touched.

It was a bright, hot day and so the doors of the stores and beer halls were open to let air circulate. The juke boxes blared music which blended with outbursts of laughter from men who, even at the early hour, were already intoxicated. My father mused aloud, but really to himself, about why there was a large number of people in town on a weekday.

My father held my hand as we entered the general store. The smell of fresh fruit, cookies baking, and coffee being ground from beans swirled about to form a delicious aroma. Even today when I go into a grocery store the beautiful odors remind me of the fear and excitement of trips to town as a child. While in the store, we learned the reason for the crowds of people in town. There was to be a hanging on the courthouse lawn at two o'clock.

In the beer hall next door we learned the details. Some man had killed his wife and her lover. He came home one night when he was supposed to be working in another county, placed twelve sticks of dynamite under the tiny shack where he lived, and blew both the people inside into eternity. The man who told my father covered his mouth to prevent me from hearing some of the sordid details. I did not really understand what the man meant when he laughingly said, "He blew 'em up right while they were doin' it."

The crowd was now gathering on the courthouse lawn. The beer halls were emptying and some stores were putting up closed signs. My father took me back to the parking lot and told me to stay in the car until he returned.

It was not my practice to disobey my father, but the excitement was too enticing. No sooner was he out of sight than I began to venture slowly toward the courthouse which was about 100 yards away and the center of the excitement. I watched my father work his way to the top of the courthouse steps, a vantage point to see the events about to take place at the Hanging Tree. It also gave me the ability to see him at all times, which meant that I had ample time to return to the parking lot the moment he headed in that direction.

I climbed the two steps at the base of the Confederate soldier's monument so I could see across the road. There was a platform on the courthouse lawn, obviously recently built because the lumber was still bright and new. It had been constructed under one of the huge limbs of the elm tree. It was a simple structure, a deck on top of four posts, with a stairway leading to the platform. In the center of the deck there was a trapdoor, which, even in my youthful naivete, I could tell was designed to be released by a lever on the side of the structure.

I was beginning to piece it all together in my mind. The man I had heard about was going to be made to stand on that trap door. The noose hanging above the platform would be put around his neck and the trapdoor beneath him released. I wondered to myself if it would hurt him. I wondered why he could not run away. Whatever the answers to my questions,

I had a clear view of the platform. I would be able to get some answers because I could see everything very well.

I kept a close eye on my father, and anytime he seemed to turn in my direction, which wasn't often because to see the gallows meant his back was to me, I hunkered down behind the base of the statue. Suddenly, everyone seemed to turn my way. I dashed behind the statue, panicked by the thought of discovery and totally dumbfounded about why everyone was interested in my whereabouts.

I soon learned they weren't looking at me. The jail where the condemned man was kept was on the opposite side of the town square from the courthouse. A squad of deputy sheriffs was bringing the prisoner to the Hanging Tree and they would pass on the walkway right in front of me. I was scared motionless.

The prisoner was a gaunt, frail-looking man in bib overalls and a frayed, white shirt. His eyes were hollow and his skin pale as his shirt. His ankles were manacled together with a very short chain so that his steps were quick and choppy as the guards led him on. The quick steps made him appear to be toe dancing. I could see why running away was impossible.

A heavy chain was taut around his waist and his wrists were gripped by cuffs attached to the chain. This held his fists tight against his stomach. I wondered to myself what would happen if he fell. He could not extend his arms to catch himself. Another chain was attached to the front of the waist chain and this was handcuffed to the deputy who led the prisoner. Two deputies with shotguns walked behind him. Behind them was the "High" sheriff, the man who, by law, had to pull the lever or pay someone else to do it.

The look of panic on the prisoner's face was an image no feeling person could ever forget. He whimpered as he shuffled along; mucous ran down out of his nostrils. The crowd that was gaily awaiting the show fell silent as the star of the show came onto the scene.

The sheriff and his deputies paused for a moment at the

bottom of the stairs leading to the platform. A couple of people, probably family members, stepped forward for just a moment.

The prisoner started to moan and whimper. The sheriff tugged at his chain to start him up the steps. It was no use to resist and the prisoner sensed the futility. He couldn't move his hands or arms and he could barely move his feet. The only choice was to do what his guards commanded. Watching this, I had a sudden feeling of claustrophobia go over me like the time I crawled under the house and became temporarily trapped in a tight place and thought for an instant I could not get free again.

The prisoner went up the stairs pulled by the two deputies, followed by the sheriff and a preacher. The noose was tightened around the condemned man's neck. His moaning got louder. He seemed to be repeating, "Oh, my God. Oh, my God."

The murmuring of the crowd which had begun as the prisoner passed suddenly stopped, making his moaning seem louder. The preacher put his hand on the prisoner's shoulder but he didn't seem to notice—he just kept moaning. The sheriff pulled the lever. I had to turn away. By now I was trembling. There was a sound like a dry stick breaking when you step on it in the woods and the crowd suddenly gave a noise like a cheer, but different. I ran toward the parking lot and threw myself in the back seat of the car. I pretended to be asleep with my face turned toward the back of the seat when my father returned.

Many times, over five decades since that event, I have relived it in my mind: the frightened prisoner, the sad-faced sheriff, the crowd of spectators. It seems unreal that these events really occurred. Public hangings have given way to the electric chair with only a small group of witnesses. The Hanging Tree remains to remind a few of us.

I felt so sorry for this prisoner that day, but as the years passed, I grew more sorry for the sheriff. The prisoner's feelings could be pure hate of an unfair system or sorrow that he was caught and had to pay for his crime. The sheriff had to deal with the worst feeling of all. He had to kill a man but could never know for sure whether or not he was guilty.

A Measure of Manhood

It is hard to describe the feeling of power and confidence it gave me to have my very own rifle. It wasn't brand new and it wasn't a high-powered deer rifle. It was a .22 caliber Winchester single shot, but it was enough to make me a man. At age twelve, I had not been allowed to hunt with the men. My experience consisted of shooting at tin cans those few times when my uncles or brothers let me fire their guns for practice. Now my weeks of saving had paid off. I had my very own gun.

I liked the heft of it as I walked slowly through the frozen grass which cracked under my feet. The November cold caused me to change hands as I cradled the rifle under my arm. I was rabbit hunting. Too young to need a hunting license, I had pinned one on from last year which I had found discarded in the tool shed.

The likelihood of my hitting a running rabbit with a rifle was remote, but I was not ready to admit that. The one cottontail which I jumped was out of sight before I fired my first shot. I reloaded and fired two more times toward where the rabbit had disappeared, just to feel like a hunter. The cold weather of Maryland in November sent me home, but not before I shot at a knot on a tree and several other inanimate objects.

I wiped the gun clean that night and counted my supply of long rifle bullets. "Dangerous within a mile," the box read.

The sticky paraffin felt good on my fingers as I sorted the bullets in neat rows on my dresser. I worked on my hunting license with a crayon to try to change the date from last year to this. I felt like a strong man, a hunter.

Every day after school and all morning on Saturday I went hunting. Hunting but not finding might be a better way to describe my level of success. My heart leaped as I fired at squirrels after they sprang out of sight. Groundhogs somehow sensed my presence and scurried back inside their dens. I was doing a lot of hunting, but thus far with nothing in the way of kills to show for my efforts.

My feeling of lack of success was largely self-imposed. My father was not a hunter and other family members did not know about my daily excursions. But guns are for killing and I was feeling more and more frustrated about my lack of success. I would lie for hours in the grass watching the groundhog den, only to pull off a premature shot when one little face appeared. Shooting pine cones on the way home did not satisfy the hunter's needs.

The pressure to kill was growing. I saw other people bringing in their bag limit of rabbits and squirrels and I knew I did not have even one kill. The feel of the rifle and the smell of expended bullets were no longer enough. I had to succeed as a hunter.

This compelling feeling was to be satisfied unexpectedly as I walked from the groundhog dens one evening. I was walking along a cow path around a hill when I saw him off just to the right of the path. It was a brush rabbit, smaller than a cottontail and much darker in color. They weren't very good to eat and they were not the sport of cottontails because they were slow and relatively dumb. These facts did not diminish my enthusiasm. My heart beat fast as I saw the nesting rabbit that didn't see me. This was a chance to make my first kill because this was a stationary target, a nesting bunny.

I stopped in my tracks and gently lifted the rifle. I held my breath to keep from being discovered. Down the V sight I could see the sleeping rabbit, nesting in a clump of dry grass. I carefully aimed the rifle to hit the hulk of the small creature. I wasn't proud. No head shots here to protect the edible portions. I wanted a kill of any kind to brag about.

I squeezed the trigger and felt a lurch against my shoulder. A puff of blue smoke appeared in front of the barrel and the rabbit leaped high into the air and then fell to earth. By the time I rushed to him he was trembling and bleeding to death from a wound in the neck. As I peered down at him, his trembling stopped and he lay silent with his eyes wide open. At first I felt elation—my first kill, even though it was cowardly done. Then I suddenly felt a great sorrow. Those piercing eyes . . . it was as if this little rabbit was asking me, "Why? Why did you kill me? Did I ever do anything to harm you? Was I a threat to you in any way?"

My plan had always been to take home any game I killed, but somehow this seemed inappropriate. I left the rabbit there to rot in the field. I walked home with the picture of the dead creature foremost in my mind.

I didn't tell anyone what had happened. I think my mother noticed a change in my attitude but she did not question why I became too busy to go hunting again. She probably knew something had happened because she could read me so well. She left me alone to sort out whatever it was that was bothering me. I spent many sleepless hours staring at the innocent face of that poor little bush hare. The question always returned but I had no good answers.

"Why did you kill me? Were you hungry like the wild dogs who frequent the hills, the wild dogs that kill only for food?"

I put the rifle away and never used it again. I moved it to my home when I married, but it remained in the closet. Over the years my family moved several times. The packers on that first move wrapped the rifle carefully for the trip. It has not been necessary to repack the rifle on the other moves over the last twenty years because it was never unpacked after the first time.

The Mysterious Hog Disease

Jed Platt was the best hog grower in the county. That's a big statement when you consider that most farmers in our county raised hogs. But every year at market time, Jed would ship a load of hogs that brought the very top price. His animals had big, hefty shoulders and thighs and long, lean flanks that yielded huge slabs of bacon, or pork bellies, as they were called.

There were various theories about how Jed always produced such prize animals, but these had to remain as speculation because Jed was not the kind who talked very much. He was a tall, lean, hard-working farmer who would barely give you the time of day, much less indulge in conversation about theories of hog raising.

Some people even went so far as to say that Jed slopped his hogs after dark each day so that people riding by his farm would not see what he fed them. The truth was that Jed and his wife worked the little farm all alone, and it was nighttime before he could get around to feeding the hogs, which was the last chore of the day. If there was any secret to his success, it was the fact that he didn't skimp on what he fed his animals. While other farmers would give them garbage and corn stalks with the ears removed, Jed gave them bundles of corn stalks, ears and all. He provided salt blocks for them to lick, and there was a little stream that ran through his pens, providing a constant source of fresh water. For the big meal, the hogs were given troughs full of fresh milk with heaps of ground corn mixed in. Jed did right by his hogs and at market time his hogs did right by him.

There was a cool nip in the September air as Jed prepared to feed his hogs one evening. He had milked his cows, poured the whole milk into the separator, and waited as the cream poured out through one nozzle and the skimmed milk out another. The cream would be shipped to a creamery and the milk mixed with ground corn for the hogs.

Jed took his eight-cell flashlight down off the shelf and started to pull the wagon loaded with a barrel of slop down the short path to the pig pen. He thought to himself, "I'll swill these hogs, then get my dinner and get to bed, because daylight is going to come early."

When he got to the pig pen, he expected the noisy hogs to be screaming for their dinner. But instead there were some strange sounds, and no hogs present at the trough. He flashed the light around the pen and his jaw dropped and his eyes opened wide at the sight before him. Some of the hogs were lying down, moaning. Some were trying to walk, but in a very unsteady way. Some were flat on their backs, with their legs sticking straight up in the air, and kicking like they were trying to walk on air. Jed dropped the handle to the wagon and looked closer, but the more he saw, the more he was alarmed. There was something dreadfully wrong with his hogs, and this could spell economic doom and social embarrassment at the next stock auction.

Jed ran back to the house and headed straight for the telephone, refusing to stop and explain to his wife, who sensed that something was very wrong. Jed fumbled through the telephone book, cursing the fact that there was so little light in the room and that telephone books were printed in such small letters. In desperation, he yelled for the operator and told her that he had to speak to Doc Sample right away. In a small Maryland town in the 1940's, telephone operators were not surprised at such a request. The new dial phones were catching on pretty well, but some of the older people still looked to the operator to directly handle emergencies. Since there was only one medical doctor and one veterinarian in the area, all Jed would have had to say was, "Get me the vet. It's an emergency."

Jed was more than a little perturbed when he learned that Doc Sample was already out on a call in the far northwest part of the county. Mrs. Sample reassured him, "We have a young veterinarian here from Maryland University who is doing his training under Dr. Sample. I'll be glad to send him out right away."

Jed was skeptical, but he had little choice. He certainly wasn't ready to have some whippersnapper practicing on his prize hogs, but even a little knowledge might be better than none at all. Reluctantly, he told Mrs. Sample to get that young veterinarian out here and double fast.

Jed was standing there, flashlight in hand, when the young vet drove up in his 1934 Dodge coupe. Jed eyed him warily as he stepped out of his car and extended his hand. "Hello there, Mr. Platt. I'm Dr. Rod Peterson and I work with Dr. Sample. I understand you have some trouble with your hogs."

Jed extended his hand, but he didn't answer the doctor directly. Rather, he muttered under his breath, "Rod Peterson, what a hell of a name for a veterinarian." He paused for a moment and looked at the young man in the beam of his flashlight, as if he were contemplating whether or not to turn this neophyte loose on his prize hogs.

The momentary standoff ended as Jed said, "Get your bag, boy. It's this way down to the pig pens."

The young man opened the rumble seat of his car and took out his bag, and the two headed quickly down the path toward the suffering patients. They made an interesting contrast of characters: Jed was a tall, thin man in bib overalls, gaunt and worn from years of hard farm labor. His dishevelled and unkempt hair and clothes contrasted with the young vet in sports shirt and slacks, rolled up over white bucks.

When they arrived at the pens, Jed shined his flashlight on one of the hogs lying close to the feeding trough. Rod climbed over the fence and knelt beside an ailing animal. He opened his bag and took out his stethoscope and thermometer and proceeded to examine the groaning hog. There was a most quizzical look on his face as he grabbed Jed's flashlight and headed toward another of the prostrate animals. He repeated the examination on several of the hogs and then stood and scratched his head as if he were pondering some great thoughts.

"Mr. Platt, you've got some very sick animals here. I've got to take some cultures and take these back to my lab. If I'm not mistaken, this is a rare disease that somehow has mysteriously reached your brood. I studied it in veterinary school, but I've never seen an actual case. I'm afraid you might lose all of them."

Jed was shocked into disbelief. "You mean I might have to kill these hogs? Are you crazy, man? Ain't there something you can do?"

"I can't be sure until I run these cultures. But, in the meantime, I'm going to put your place under quarantine. I don't want any animals coming in contact with these hogs if they've got what I think they have. I'm going to put this sign up on your gate as I leave, and you make sure that you don't take any of these animals out of here. I'll talk with the county agent, and if we have to kill your hogs he'll pay you something for them. I'll get back with you first thing in the morning."

Jed didn't sleep much that night and he didn't know what he would really find when he went out the next morning. Once again, there was a sight that he couldn't believe. All of the animals were up, moving around, and obviously hungry. He hesitated for a moment, wondering whether or not he should spend money on hogs that would have to be destroyed that very same day. But he gave in to their pleading for food. He checked the barrel of slop to be sure the cool air had kept it from spoiling, then poured it into the trough. All of the pigs ate heartily. He went back to the house to wait for the report which would settle the fate of his brood and determine his economic situation for the months to come.

Jed was still anxious and deep in thought as he walked from the barn after milking. His emotions were mixed as he saw Doc Sample and young Rod Peterson drive up in front of his house. They exchanged a mumbled greeting and headed down toward the pig pens. Jed didn't share the fact that the hogs were up moving around and taking food because he thought that might just be a phase of this terrible disease, and the animals would have to be killed anyway.

There was a look of relief in the old veterinarian's eyes as they saw the pigs frolicking around rather than lying down as they had expected. Rod was explaining to Doc Sample that the cultures would not be ready until later in the day, but Doc Sample didn't seem to pay much attention. Instead, he crossed the fence and patted a couple of pigs on the head, and looked at them with his experienced eye. He then gazed around and lifted up his nose like he was sniffing the air. He moved toward the small stream that was running through the pig pens, lifted his hat off his head with one hand, and proceeded to scratch his head with the other. He leaned down and dipped his hand into the mud beside the stream and touched a finger to his tongue. A big smile came across his face.

As he stood up and walked back toward the young veterinarian and the anxious farmer, he announced that the hogs were all right. "There's no disease. These hogs just have a big hangover, that's all. Just keep on feeding them like you have been and you'll have a fine sale when the auction comes around." Jed and the young veterinarian didn't understand what old Doc Sample meant. But he explained himself as they walked back toward the car.

By sundown that day, everybody in the county knew what had happened and it caused more amusement than anyone had seen for a long time. Even to this day people laugh when you talk about the great, mysterious hog disease that hit Jed Platt's brood back in 1941.

It seems that just upstream from Jed's place, there was a wood that was part of the Dobson farm. The Dobson boys, like most everybody back in that time, had themselves a still where they turned out huge quantities of corn liquor. Ordinarily, when the sheriff was about ready to raid a still, the word got out well in advance. By the time he arrived with his deputies, all that remained was a clearing in the wood or maybe a few empty vats. But somehow the Dobson boys hadn't gotten the word. When the sheriff arrived, there were 80 gallons of prime liquor which had been freshly distilled and another ten gallons were in the making. Much to the displeasure of everybody around, including the sheriff, the fresh liquor was

dumped out, down the hill into the stream that ran right down to Jed Platt's place. The hogs had gotten a whiff of that fresh corn and they couldn't resist. They indulged themselves in the stream and became so drunk they couldn't stand up. The mysterious hog disease was really a good dose of high grade moonshine.

Fortunately, young Rod Peterson was only in the county on temporary assignment with Doc Sample. When his internship was finished he went off to practice his profession in another state, where the story of the mysterious hog disease would not follow him. Jed Platt shrugged off the situation and went back to raising prize hogs. But the people of Montgomery County, Maryland, never stopped talking about the incident. It was just too good to let go of so they embellished it and are doing so to this day.

All you have to do is get several of those old-timers together and they'll tell you what happened over at Jed Platt's place after the hogs got drunk on that moonshine. They'll tell you how the Baptist preacher went over and converted them hogs so that they would never drink again. They'll tell you about the young deputy sheriff that went over there and gave one of them hogs a ticket for drunken walkin'. They'll tell you about the Methodists who tried to buy up the hogs because they figured their meat would make some powerful gravy.

Of course, none of those stories is true. Neither is it true that the Dobson boys retrieved some of their brew after it ran through the pig pen and sold it to a major distillery which uses the formula in one of the prime whiskeys to this day.

POETRY

I Can, If You Think I Can

You asked me can I do it? Well, don't you understand?
You're the one to answer because I can if YOU think
    I can.
I have the courage and the skill, but these alone
    won't do.
I must be sure that you believe I can do what you ask
    me to.
So, whether or not I reach my goals, in your hand I
    place the key.
Before I can ever reach the heights, I must know YOU
    believe in me.

The Enemy Inside

There's an enemy out to get you; he'll destroy you if
    he can.
His name is Lack of Confidence and he's lurking in
    every man.
Whenever you face a challenge, he will whisper in
    your ear
And tell you all the risks involved, and the things that
    you should fear.
But there's one sure way to defeat him: it's to
    constantly say "I can!"
To know in your heart, from the very start, you're
    equal to any man.

Then you venture when others are timid, see hope
    when others despair.
You rely on yourself, you don't give up, you fight hard
    and long and fair.
You don't spend your time complaining about luck—
    how it passed you by.
And you don't make any excuses for the times that you
    just didn't try.
This positive way of thinking gives a key that will set
    you free;
While the mass of men stand idly by, your dreams are
    realities.

Perspective

I had to walk to town that day, a long and rugged
    road.
This angered me and it hurt my feet, for I shouldered
    a heavy load.
And then I saw a little boy with a crutch where one
    leg should be.
He stood alone on the schoolhouse lawn and he smiled
    as he waved to me.
I smiled through tears as I raised my hand and
    continued on with my chore,
But my feet didn't hurt, though I quickened my pace,
    and the road wasn't rough anymore.

A dazzling sunset bathed the sky at the end of a summer
    day.
Preoccupied, I gave but a glance and started to turn
    away.
It's only a sunset, is that so great? I've seen a thousand
    or more.

Then a blind man beside me said, "Tell me, friend, are
    the colors as bright as before?"
As I described to a sightless man the things he could not
    see,
The awesome beauty I would have missed was no
    longer hidden from me.
Lord, let me know the message these events are meant to
    give.
I must show that I am grateful by the loving way I
    live,
Not complaints and petty grievances for the bumps and
    scrapes of life,
Not enlarging little problems till they loom like major strife.
When I'm adding up the balance, it must come as no
    surprise.
I have reasons to be joyous—I have legs and I have
    eyes.

Until I Believe In Me

God gave me many talents and a choice of what I
    can be.
But I will amount to nothing unless I can believe
    in me.
He gave strength to my arms and a brain to use and
    visions for me to see,
But my dreams will be empty wishes until I can
    believe in me.

He gave me the love and strong support of friends and
    a family.
But these will all be wasted unless I can believe in me.
So let me live life boldly—not boastful, but eagerly—
Deserving of others' faith and trust because first
    I BELIEVED IN ME.

Margin of Victory

Who decides what your fate will be
When you play this game called Life?
Who determines the final score
Gives victory, or merely strife?
Have the outcomes all been ordered?
Are we puppets on a string?
Or does our Maker gave a choice
Of results our life will bring?

No, the winners have not been chosen,
But the rules have been firmly set.
We must determine the final score
And the trophies we will get.
The world is a great arena
For the one with the will to win.
Success and acclaim will surely come . . .
If we conquer defeat within.

But the difference? It's in our striving,
And what we think we can be.
Because the will to win the game of Life
Is the margin of victory.

I Remember Him Now

I remember him now—a shy little boy who sat in the
     back of my class.
He never talked; he did his work just barely enough to pass.
He never tried to play the clown, nor did he seek my aid.
It haunts me when I think about the difference I might
     have made.

The principal said I'd be the one to tell his family.
A suicide note addressed to no one simply said:
     "I've got to be free."
"Why," I protested, "should I be charged to bring the
     horrible news?
I hardly knew him. I taught him, yes, but there are
     others you should choose."

"It's because of this note that we found in his things
     that we ask you to be the one.
The memory book that the dime store gives and the
     kids find so much fun—
He only wrote on a single page, that pathetic little
     creature.
He wrote your name on the page that says:
     THIS IS MY FAVORITE TEACHER."

Now, Teacher, I Understand

I came from a world where you have to fight for
    everything you gain.
Where people are cruel and you use your fists to give
    them back the same.
But you said, "Be kind!" and I was confused. Why
    should I give a helping hand?
Then you brought my homework when I was sick.
    Now, teacher, I understand.

Whenever I trusted anyone, they always let me down.
So I kept to myself—I risked no friends—and I
    shielded myself with a frown.
But you accepted the note I gave, though written in my
    own hand,
And you smiled and hugged me when I confessed.
    Now, teacher, I understand.

I never thought I mattered much to anyone on earth.
In fact, at times, I hated myself for having so little
    worth.
Then I realized that you truly cared. It wasn't an act or
    sham.
The tear in your eye on the last day of school—
    Now, teacher, I understand.

That's What I Need To Know

You taught me how to read the words, to spell them
      and write them down.
You showed me the rules for a paragraph and how
      poetry should sound.
But you didn't tell me what to say when bigotry starts
      to show,
When words express hate and prejudice. Now that's
      what I need to know!

You taught me about arithmetic, how numbers are
      so exact.
You taught me equations and how they are solved with
      precise mathematical facts.
But you didn't tell of my fellow man and the debt that
      I might owe.
What share must I give to the helpless poor? Now
      that's what I need to know!

The facts and figures you gave me are but tools that I
      can use
As instruments of help or hurt, depending on how I
      choose.
My youth puts me at your mercy, and the bent of my
      life will show:
Did you give mere information, or all the things that I
      need to know?

Escape

Give me a field on a windy day,
A grassy field in which to stray,
A kite to raise up in the air
And let me do my dreaming there.
The gentle touch of sun and breeze
My troubled heart and spirit frees
And fills a need so deep in me
To rise above reality.

The Fish That Couldn't Swim

This peculiar story that I relate
Has a beginning that's rather grim.
It's a story of strife,
Of a fish and his wife,
And their baby who couldn't swim.
They took him down to the water's edge
And pushed him off the bank.
He thrashed the water with tail and fin,
But still, he promptly sank.
He couldn't play with the other fish
As they frolicked and swam in the lake.
Even the thought of taking a bath
Made his whole body shiver and shake.

And then one day he climbed a tree
To watch the boats go by.
The limb gave way, and he started to fall
And to his surprise he could fly!
His mother and father were filled with joy
And the animals cheered aloud.
To have a fish that could fly with the birds . . .
It made the whole fish neighborhood proud!
So if you try a certain task
And you don't do as well as you wish,
Don't give up. Try another job.
You may be a Flying Fish!

The Gloom Of Winter

The chill of damp fog pierces my clothing
And penetrates my soul.
Winter casts a mood of melancholy
As I stand amid barren trees and brown lifeless grass.
The grey sky sinks low, as if burdened
By the weight of impending snow.
Houses are sealed tight and wrapped in a garland
        of ice.
The joy of early winter is faded,
Like the Christmas carols and the New Year's greetings.
The monotony of short, cold days wears on
With no sign of relief.
The whole world stoops in mental depression.

Somewhere a hyacinth shelters its first blossom
From the smothering snow.
And somewhere a winged harbinger of spring
Starts on a long trip north.
But just now, this is too remote
To save me from the gloom of winter.

A Christmas Elegy

The Christmas presents are opened,
Then quietly put away.
There is no laughter, no shouts of joy
So typical of the day.
Mother and Dad try hard to smile
To bravely hold back a tear,
But one little stocking hangs empty
On the fireplace this year.

A faithful puppy, with ears erect,
Waits by the kitchen door.
He wants his master to come and play,
Like so many times before.
The house so quiet a ticking clock
Is like thunder to the ear.

One little stocking hangs empty
On the fireplace this year.

The snow still gently falling,
The winter daylight ends.
A flickering candle makes a glow
Like a halo around its head.
The tiny face in the picture frame
Smiles impish, yet truth is clear.
One little stocking hangs empty
On the fireplace this year.

The clothes once worn by a little boy
Can be carefully stored away.
His toys can be shared with the other kids,
So unselfish, he'd want it that way.
And Christmas sometime may be happy again,
And there may be laughter and cheer.
But one little stocking hangs empty
On the fireplace this year.

Home To Emptiness

The traffic keeps its snail-like pace,
Thwarting my efforts to regain those minutes
Lost in the faceless routines
Which turn the hope of my day into frustration.
My work done, at least in name,
The very salvation of my sanity
Rests upon those heavenly words,
"Daddy, it's so good to have you home.
Tell me the story about . . . "

The last obstacle complete, I take the stairs in threes.
Glancing at my watch, I dash to her room,
To the one sure haven from all defeat.
"I'm sorry, Dad. She tried to wait for you.
She even cried a little, hoping you would come.
But now she's asleep."

The thrill of home turns to emptiness.

The Prisoner

The solitary prisoner sits peering into the black
    darkness of his cell.
His eyes strain for a ray of light to pierce the tiny
    window far above him.
The pain of shackles on his gaunt arms and legs
    reminds him that his wretched existence
In this damp, stenchful hell will have no end, save
    death.
In this infinity of despair there is but one hope: That
    moment each day when the sun defies
The tree that shadows the window. For this fleeting
    instant there is light
And life and hope, and reprieve from tortuous
    darkness.
The prisoner sits staring, Not knowing whether it is
    night or day.
Is the light soon to come? Or has his fevered mind
    betrayed him?
Has the precious moment passed? And then, the most
    agonizing thought of all:
Will clouds hold back the sun and forbid even this
    brief glimpse of life?
Oh Death! Take me now, if this is so.

The Autumn Reflections

The cool breeze of autumn touches my face
    And comforts my longing.
I look upon the water, now cold and barren of life.
Memory quickens, and the thoughts of you
    And summer rush over me.
The beach is still, save only for the tide
    Splashing upon the shore.
The memory of your laughter, your winsome smile,
Haunt me like a pleasant specter from the past.
Was it only a dream? Did you ever really exist?
Am I mad? Could a memory so beautiful be only
The remnants of cruel fantasy?
I must not dwell upon reality,
Lest reason overcome ecstasy.
I must hold you in my heart forever.
Even truth cannot rob me.
Time and distance and change must yield to my passion.
There can be no autumn in my life, though summer
    be gone.

Smoke Dreams

My world is quiet as I gaze
    Into the flickering flame before me,
The fireplace, once aglow, now quiets
    Like the sighing of my heart.
My passion ebbs, and the flame that started brisk
    Flutters, and disappears.
The thought of never having you punishes me.
    Hope that once rushed like the blazing fire
Dies, as I sit alone in the darkness.
    A tiny wisp of smoke rises unseen to seek the night.
In my solitude I accept the reality
    Of life without you.

Strangers

A boy, a girl, strangers on a beach, one step apart, and yet,
Separated by a whole world of tradition.
They must not speak, lest they violate the rules of society
Which govern strangers.
A lonely boy, a lonely girl. One step apart.
A casual meeting of their eyes, then both turn away quickly
To hide any show of interest.
Could she be the one to share my life,
To provide the missing part of me?
Would she encourage me, ease my fears, love me?
Is she on fire with the same passion
That haunts my solitary life?
She stares aimlessly toward the ocean,
Feeling the same pain and pondering the same questions.
Does he see me? Would he like to hold and caress me?
Could he be the father for my children?
Each waits with the hope that somehow their lives
     will touch.
Each waits, imprisoned by the fear of beginning.
The day ends, and a boy and a girl leave the beach, slowly,
Hoping that yet some way will come for them to meet.
     But no.
One reluctant step becomes two, And three, and . . .
Tomorrow, far apart, and never to meet again,
Memories will begin to fade and heal the hurt
Of two strangers on a beach.

Constant Companion

The list of persons that I call friend, through the years
    I will modify.
This winding path that we call life brings change
    which I can't deny.
But there is one person I can't escape, whether friend
    or foe to me.
When I stare at the face in the looking glass, it's the
    one I will always see.

No secret place that I can hide, no disguise that I can
    wear,
Each moment that I sleep or wake, the same small
    space we'll share.
I can choose companions or solitude, I can socialize or
    be free,
But there is one person I can't elude: There is no
    escaping me.

So, what kind of person shall I choose to be with
    every day?
The one who will know of my every deed who will
    hear every word I say?
He must be someone gentle and kind who forgives
    rather easily,
One who doesn't nag me for my faults, one who looks
    for the good in me.

Sleep, My Daughter

Sleep, little girl, the deep and peaceful sleep that only
    innocence can bring.
Here among the toys in your happy room, let me be
    with you and sense the contentment of your
    world.

With your hand still clasping mine, I close the book,
    the story half told.
You know it so well, the happy ending, the funny
    rhyme that makes you laugh long before I say it.

If only your life would remain this simple.
If only I could protect you from the world and
    growing up.
I cannot. There will be pain and tears far deeper than
    the brief hurt of a bump or a skinned knee that is
    the extent of your young experience.

Someone will hurt your heart—that is inevitable.
You will learn of terror in the world, and fear and evil.
You will learn that all men are not good, that stories
    don't always end happily.
You will learn the art of polite deceit required by
    society.
You will learn to hide your doubt about religion, and
You will learn to harbor thoughts which cannot be
    shared with anyone.
You will learn disappointment.

But now you rest in innocence, and all these things weigh
upon my heart.

If I could only hold back the morning and the truth of life.

If only I could take these things in double measure and
leave you forever free.

I move my hands from yours and tuck the covers about your
shoulders.

Gently, gently. You must not awaken to question the tear
in my eye.

You must not know the secret cares that fathers bear.

Let me quietly leave your room, and the world where I
can but visit in the company of one as innocent as you.

I Knew You Meant It

You were young and so beautiful; I was painfully shy.
I asked you for a date, And you said you weren't
interested.
I was disappointed because
I knew you meant it.

Time passed and I asked you again. You said yes and
we had a good time.
You told me I was the one you loved,
And I was so happy because
I knew you meant it.

The day we married we pledged to love forever.
Based on that pledge, we built a home
And raised three beautiful children.
I never feared growing old because you said we'd be
together
And I knew you meant it.

But fate changed our plans.
The simple illness I thought so trivial, you knew was
serious.
You smiled when you told me I'd have to go on alone,
But you chilled my soul because
I knew you meant it.

The Eyes of Christ

I searched for Christ in the eyes of men.
My seeking was all in vain.
I found no call upon my heart
That the Son of God would claim.
Even the eyes of a holy man,
A God-like man, they said,
Only reflected a shallow faith,
No path to a cross had led.
My quest abandoned, I dropped my gaze
To a humble beggar's eye.
The Christ I sought reached out to me.
I could not pass him by.
Those ancient words came rushing back,
And I fell upon my knees.
"You'll find Me when you seek to help
The very least of these."

My Quest

I searched for peace on the mountain top
But there was no peace in my soul.
I found it not in the meadow glen
Or the gentle ocean roll.
And then, in a frightening thunderstorm
I saw a little bird,
Perched calm in the bend of a mighty tree
As if he never heard.
The answer came clear,
My quest was done:
Peace isn't a place apart.
It's the simple knowledge that God exists.
It abounds in a faithful heart.

The Deserted Church

The little church upon the hill
Is weather-beaten, worn;
A simple place, now left unused—
A new one has been born.
But still it has a certain air
The new one cannot claim,
An air of righteous dignity
That logic can't explain.
Lord, help me see the lesson
As I seek to know Your will.
Help me see what they abandoned
In the church upon the hill.
Gaudy spires and great cathedrals
Have no base in Your command.
They are structures filled with emptiness,
Idols built by foolish man.

Revelation

Have you ever savored the twilight
Or walked through a meadow glen
Just as the sun is going down
And day is at its end?
The parting rays of sunlight
Paint a scene on the western sky
That makes the greatest works of man
Seem but an alibi.
Take heed and know the meaning.
It's more than a poet's verse.
This scene reveals to every man
The Lord of the Universe.

Dialogue

Nature's voice is calling.
It's varied wails we hear:
The cry of grass at morning
For the sun to dry its tear;
The pleading of an errant stream
That can't o'erleap its wall;
The quiet sobs of fading flowers
As twilight cloaks the mall.
Yes, Nature needs our giddy feet
To stumble o'er her breast,
To find enchantment in the nooks
That break the gentle crests,
To hear the sounds not meant for ears,
The sounds no voice imparts,
The whispered utterance of God
That's heard within the heart.

Books By
IVAN FITZWATER

Loving Parents/Happy Kids
A Team Approach to Child-Rearing

Time Under Control
Efficient Self-Management In and Out
of the Office

Laugh With Me/Cry With Me
Inspiration, Pathos, and Humor

You Can Be A Powerful Leader
The Secrets of Powerful Leadership

Failproof Children
A Guide to Positive Parenting

These books may be ordered from:

Management Development Institute, Inc.
P.O. Box 791276
San Antonio, Texas 78279-1276